TH~~E~~
T~~HE LILY~~
A JACOB BOEHME READER

Edited by Wayne Kraus

For

Jacob Boehme Online

http://jacobboehmeonline.com

Copyright©2014, by Kraus House

Cover art and interior illustrations, copper engravings from *Alle Theosophische Schrifften*, by Jacob Böhme, Amsterdam, 1682. Artist: Jan Luycken

Table of Contents

I. OVERTURE 1

II. TESTIMONY 3

   From EPISTLE 2 3

   THE THIRD EPISTLE. 7

   A LETTER TO ABRAHAM VON SOMMERFELD, CONCERNING THE BOOK *AURORA*; 7

   AURORA Chapter 19 Concerning *Heaven*. 22

   From EPISTLE 1 28

   From *APOLOGIA: BALTHAZAR TILCKEN* 30

III. ANTICHRIST 32

   THE THREEFOLD LIFE OF MAN chapter 11 32

   The Great Open Gate of the Antichrist 32

   THE TENTH EPISTLE. Of the Killing of Antichrist in Ourselves. 42

   From THE WAY TO CHRIST, part three, The New Creation, chapter seven 49

   Compilation from THE LIFE AND DOCTRINE OF JACOB BOEHME by Franz Hartmann, chapter one ... 51

IV. FAITH 55

   THE INCARNATION OF CHRIST: THE THIRD TREATISE 55

   CHAPTER I 55

   WHAT FAITH IS, AND HOW IT IS ONE SPIRIT WITH GOD 55

   CHAPTER II 57

OF THE ORIGIN OF FAITH, AND WHY FAITH AND DOUBT DWELL TOGETHER 57

CHAPTER III..61

OF THE PROPERTY OF FAITH, HOW IT GOES OUT FROM THE WILL OF THE NATURAL CRAVING INTO THE FREEWILL OF GOD...61

CHAPTER IV 66

WHAT THE WORK OF FAITH IS AND HOW THE WILL MAY WALK THEREIN AND CONCERNING ITS GUIDE 66

CHAPTER V 71

WHY THE UNGODLY ARE NOT CONVERTED; WHICH IS THE MOST PAINFUL PART OF CONVERSION; OF THE FALSE SHEPHERDS; HOW WE MUST ENTER INTO GOD'S KINGDOM; OF THE DESTRUCTION OF THE DEVIL'S KINGDOM; OF THE THREE FORMS AND WHAT WE HAVE INHERITED FROM ADAM AND CHRIST..71

CHAPTER VI...81

WHAT LUST CAN DO; HOW WE IN ADAM HAVE FALLEN AND IN CHRIST HAVE BEEN BORN AGAIN; AND THAT IT IS NOT SUCH AN EASY MATTER TO BECOME A TRUE CHRISTIAN...81

CHAPTER VII 85

TO WHAT END THIS WORLD WITH ALL BEING WAS CREATED, ALSO CONCERNING TWO ETERNAL MYSTERIES; OF THE EXCEEDINGLY FIERCE STRUGGLE IN MAN FOR THE IMAGE, AND WHEREIN THE TREE OF THE CHRISTIAN FAITH STANDS, GROWS AND BEARS FRUIT 85

CHAPTER VIII..90

IN WHAT MANNER GOD FORGIVES SIN, AND HOW YOU BECOME A CHILD OF GOD...................................90

THE INCARNATION OF CHRIST CHAPTER XIII...94

V. OF THE SUPRASENSUAL LIFE 107

THE SUPRASENSUAL LIFE 107

DIALOGUE II...130

OF HEAVEN and HELL..150

A DIALOGUE BETWEEN A SCHOLAR AND HIS MASTER *SHOWING* w*hither the blessed and the damned Souls go when they depart from their Bodies; and How Heaven and Hell are in Man; Where the Angels and Devils dwell in this World's Time; How far Heaven and Hell are asunder; and What and Whence the Angels and Human Souls are; What the Body of Man is; and Why the Soul is capable of receiving Good and Evil; Of the Destruction of the World; Of Man's Body in and after the Resurrection; Where Heaven and Hell shall be; Of the Last Judgment; and Why the Strife in the Creature must be.*..............................150

THE WAY FROM DARKNESS TO LIGHT 174

VI. The Signature of All Things 197

Chapter VII 197

Chapter XVI 199

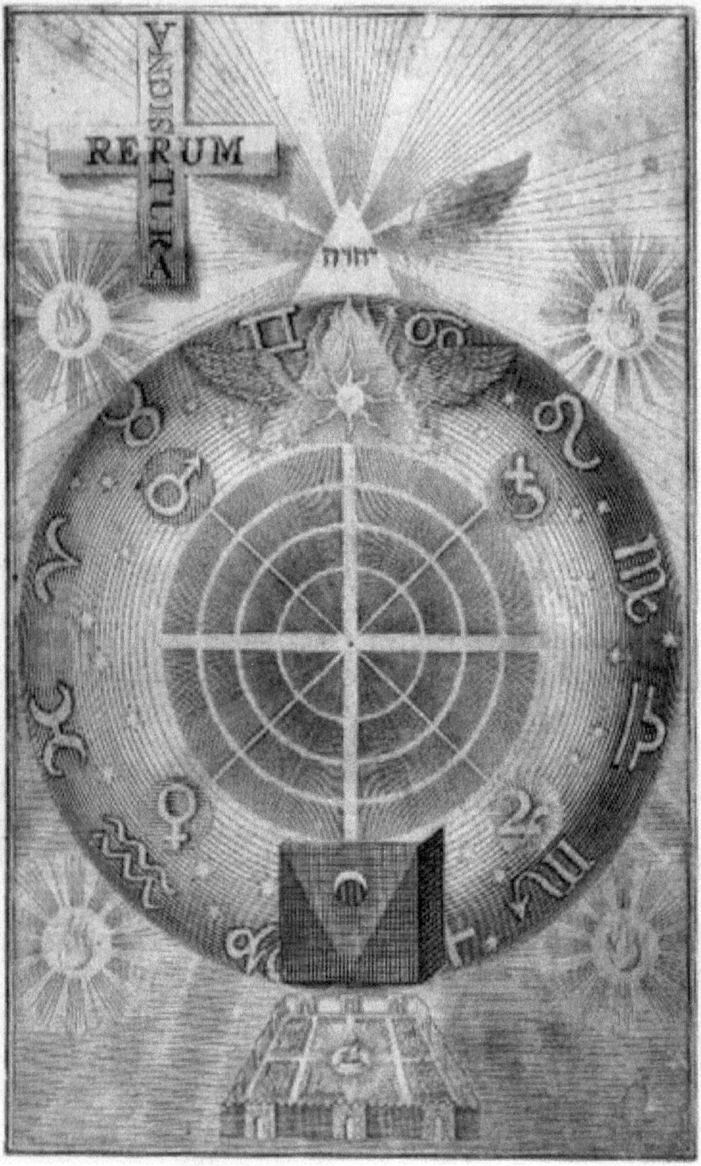
RERUM
יהוה

INTRODUCTION

This book of Jacob Boehme's essential writings follows the course of the waters of Ezekiel's Temple: ankle-deep, knee-deep, hip-deep, "waters to swim in" and finally "a river that cannot be passed over." (Ezekiel 47) It begins with the easiest of his writings and ends with selections from *The Signature of All Things*.

The Signature is the most arcane of Boehme's books, written for an audience of 17th century scientists, i.e. "Chymists," "Physicks," "Siderealists" and "Spagyromancers." To the 21st century mind it is "a quaint and curious volume of forgotten lore," written in a forgotten idiom. But to those who have ears to hear – or, as Boehme might put it, "to him whose Signature is tinctured with the Heavenly Mercury" – it is Deep calling unto Deep.

When it first appeared in English in 1651, an old Quaker said of the author, "I durst never saile into ye ocean of his vast conceits with my little skull, me thought the reading of him was like ye standing upon a precipice or by a cannon shott off, ye waft of them lickt up all my brains."

But he persisted in reading until understanding dawned, and the Quaker became a "Behmenist."

William Law said, "When I first began to read Behmen's book, it put me into a perfect sweat. But as I discerned sound truths and the glimmering of a deep ground and sense even in the passages not then clearly intelligible to me, and found myself, as it were, strongly prompted in my heart to dig in these writings, I followed this impulse with continual aspirations and persistent prayer to God for His help and divine illumination, *if I was called* to understand them. By reading in this manner again and again, and from time to time, I perceived that my heart felt well, and my understanding opened gradually; till at length I found what a treasure was hid in this field."

The Signature was my own first encounter with Boehme. I entered the River Behmen from the deep end, and nearly drowned. In the end, I too found the hidden treasure, but it took fifteen years. The purpose of this little book is to shorten the route for those who are new to Boehme or who have tried his deep writings and found them impenetrable.

William Blake said, "Allegory addressed to the Intellectual Powers while it is altogether hidden from the Corporeal Understanding, is my Definition of the Most Sublime Poetry." That is precisely the effect that Boehme's writings have on spiritually attuned but uninitiated readers. While the reasoning mind flounders in incomprehension, we are mysteriously drawn on, and persist until the Sunlight falls on the page, and deep down inside a sleeping giant awakes. That giant is Faith, and in Faith we discover a faculty of perception immeasurably higher than reason. From Boehme we learn a new way of reading, and a new way of thinking, and then graduate from thinking to direct perception. We find that where reasoning ends, revelation begins. As Coventry Patmore said, with a Solomonic flourish, "Lovers put out the candles and draw the curtains, when they wish to see the god and the goddess; and, in the higher communion, the night of thought is the light of perception."

The chapters of this book are as follows:

I. Overture

II. Testimony – autobiographical selections from his epistles and the famous 19th chapter of *Aurora*, in which he describes his own passage from darkness to light

III. Antichrist – The reason such prominence is given to this obscure topic is that it features prominently in Boehme's writings. "Antichrist," "Babel" and "the Great Whore" refer to the organized religion system. The Christian religion was, and remains, the vanguard of opposition to the gospel of Christ.

IV. Faith – a long selection from the third book of *The Incarnation of Christ*. In my own experience, this is the most illuminating of all Boehme's writings.

V. The Suprasensual Life, and two related tracts traditionally published under the title *The Way to Christ* –

VI. The Signature of All Things - selections

In Boehme, the Lily, along with the Pearl of Great Price, the Garland of Sophia and the Philosopher's Stone, is a symbol of the new birth. It is often coupled with the Rose; "the Rose in the Time of the Lily," "the paradisaical lily-twig in Christ's Garden of Roses." This is perhaps a reference to the "Bridal Chamber" of philosophical alchemy, another image of the new birth signified by the union of a red and white rose, that is, soul and spirit.

I. OVERTURE
from *The Signature of All Things*

The whole host of heaven is set and tuned into one harmony; each angelical kingdom into a peculiar instrument, but all mutually composed into one music; into the only love-voice of God. Every string of this melody exalts and rejoices the other; and it is only a mere ravishing lovely and delightful hearing.

As it was before the times of this world in his eternal harmony, so also it continues in the creaturely voice in him in his eternity; and this is the beginning and the end of all things. And since Adam had quenched the light-world, the light-world was again incorporated with the name of Jesus which came to pass in the conception of Mary. God became man, that he might again repair his glorious instrument which he had made for his praise, which perished, and would not sound according to the desire of his joy and love, and introduce again the true love-sound into the strings.

He has introduced the voice which sounds in his presence again into us, his instrument; he is become what I am, and has made me what he is, so that I may say, that I am the sound of his instrument and divine voice, at which now I rejoice in all my fellow-strings and voices, who with me are tuned and set as an eternal work, to the praise and glory of God.

Thus know ye now, my Fellow-Voices in the Praise of God, that I sound with my String played upon in the Spirit upon and in your Note, and thus sing I to you; that whatever Jesus has done through the Christ, viz. through his and my Humanity, the same he does yet today in me and in all my Fellow-Members.

The Spirit of the Lord of Hosts has out of his Love planted a new Branch in the human Property, which shall Root out the Thorns of the Devil, and make known his Child Jesus to all Nations, Tongues and Speeches, and that in the Morning of the eternal Day.

II. TESTIMONY

From EPISTLE 2

5. I will not conceal from you the simple childlike way which I walk in Christ Jesus; for I can write nothing of myself, but as of a child, which neither knows or understands anything; neither has ever been learned, but only that which the Lord vouchsafes to know in me; according to the measure, as He manifests Himself in me.

6 For I never desired to know anything of the Divine Mystery, much less understood I the way how to seek or find it; I knew nothing of it, as it is the condition of poor laymen in their simplicity, I sought only after the heart of Jesus Christ, that I might hide myself therein from the wrathful anger of God, and the violent assaults of the devil; and I besought the Lord earnestly for His holy Spirit, and His grace, that He would be pleased to bless and guide me in Him; and take away from me, anything that would turn me away from Him, and I resigned myself wholly to Him, that I might not live to my own will, but to His; and that He only might lead and direct me: to the end, that I might be His child in His Son Jesus Christ.

7. In this my earnest Christian seeking and desire (wherein I suffered many a shrewd repulse, but at last being resolved rather to put my life to utmost hazard, than to give over and leave off) the gate was opened unto me, so that in one quarter of an hour I saw and knew more than if I had been many years together at an University; at which I exceedingly marveled, and did not know how it happened to me; and I turned my heart to praise God for it

8. For I saw and knew the Being of all Beings, the Byss (the ground or original foundation), and Abyss (that which is without ground, or bottomless and fathomless); also the birth [or eternal generation] of the holy Trinity; the descent, and origin of this world, and of all creatures, through the divine wisdom; I knew and saw in myself all the three worlds; namely, the divine, angelical, and paradisiacal world, and then the dark world; being the origin of nature to the fire: And then thirdly, the external, visible world, being a procreation, or external birth; or as a substance expressed, or spoken forth, from both the internal and spiritual worlds; and I saw, and knew the whole Being [or working essence] in the evil, and in the good; and the mutual original, and existence of each of them; and likewise how the pregnant mother (*genetrix* or fruitful bearing womb of eternity) brought forth, so that I not only greatly wondered at it, but also exceedingly rejoiced.

9. And presently it came powerfully into my mind to set the same down in writing, for a memorandum to myself; albeit I could very hardly apprehend the same in my external man, and express it with the pen; yet however I must begin to labour in these great Mysteries as a child that goes to school: I saw it (as in a great deep) in the internal, for I had a thorough view of the universe as in a CHAOS, wherein all things are couched and wrapt up, but it was impossible for me to explicate and unfold the same.

10. Yet it opened itself in me from time to time, as in a young plant: albeit the same was with me for the space of twelve years, and I was as it were pregnant, (or breeding of it) with all, and found a powerful driving and instigation within me, before I could bring it forth into an external form of writing; which afterward fell upon me as a sudden shower, which hits whatever it lights upon; just

so it happened to me, whatsoever I could apprehend, and bring into the external principle of my mind the same I wrote down.

11. However, afterward the sun did shine on me a good while, but not in a continual constant manner; for when the same did hide itself, I scarce knew, or well understood my own writings, so that man must acknowledge that his knowledge is not his own, or from himself, but God's and from God; and that God knows *in* the soul of man after what manner and measure He pleases.

14. Thus now I have written, not from the instruction or knowledge received from men, not from the learning or reading of books; but I have written out of my own book which was opened in me, being the noble similitude of God, the book of the noble and precious image (understand God's own similitude or likeness) was bestowed upon me to read; and therein I have studied, as a child in the house of its mother, which beholds what the father does, and in his childlike play imitates his father; I have no need of any other book.

15. My book has only three leaves; they are the three principles of eternity, wherein I can find all whatsoever Moses and the prophets, Christ and his apostles have taught and spoken; I can find therein the foundation of the world and all mysteries; yet not I, but the spirit of God, does it according to the measure, as He pleases.

16. For I have besought, and begged of Him many hundred times, that if my knowledge did not make for His glory, and conduce to the amending and instructing (bettering or benefit) of my brethren, He would be pleased to take it from me, and preserve me only in His love; yet I found that by my praying or earnest desiring I did only enkindle the fire more strongly in me; and in such

inflammation, knowledge, and manifestation I made my writings.

17. Yet I did not intend to make myself known with them among such persons, as now I see is come to pass; I still thought I wrote for myself only, albeit the spirit of God, in the mystery of God, in my spirit, did sufficiently show me to what end it was; yet outward reason was always opposite, save only sometimes when the morning star did arise, and even then reason was also thereby enkindled, and did dance along, as if it had comprehended the pearl, yet it was far from it.

18. God dwells in the noble image, but not in the spirit of the stars and elements; He possesses nothing, save Himself only, in His own likeness; and albeit He does possess something (as, indeed, He possesses all things), yet nothing comprehends Him, but what does originally arise and spring from Him; as, namely, the soul in the similitude of God.

19. Besides, all my writings are like unto a young scholar's that is going to school; God has, according to His will, brought my soul into a wonderful school; and in truth I cannot ascribe or arrogate anything unto myself, as if my selfhood were, or understood, anything.

20. No man must conceive higher of me than he sees; for the work in my studying, or writing, is none of mine; I have it only according to the measure as the Lord is pleased to give it me; I am nothing but His instrument, whereby He effects what He wills. This I relate unto you, my beloved friends, for an instruction and information, lest any should esteem me otherwise than I am, namely, as if I were a man of high art and deep understanding and reason, for I live in weakness and infirmity, in the childhood and simplicity of Christ; and my sport and

pastime is in that childlike work which He has allotted to me; yea, I have my delight therein as in a garden of pleasure, where many noble flowers grow; and in the meantime I will joy and recreate myself therewith, till I shall again obtain the flower of Paradise in the new man.

41. We must take no thought or solicitous care what we are to know, and how we will know, but we must merely enter into the incarnation and birth of Jesus Christ, and into His suffering and death, and continually, with all willingness, tread in His footsteps and follow Him, and think that we are here only upon our pilgrim's path, where we must walk through a dangerous way, and enter again in Christ on the narrow way, into our native country, whence Adam has led us astray. In this way only lies the pearl of the *mysterium magnum* [or the jewel of the Great Mystery]—all studying, book reading, seeking, searching, and grounding [on our received principles or orthodox apprehensions] besides, and, without this way, are but dead means, and obtain not the virgin's crown [or the pearl of Sophia], but gather together heaps of thistles and thorns, which sting and gall the children of God.

THE THIRD EPISTLE.

A LETTER TO ABRAHAM VON SOMMERFELD, CONCERNING THE BOOK *AURORA*;

Light, Salvation, and Eternal Power flowing from the well-spring of Life, Jesus Christ, be our Refreshment and Comfort.

1. NOBLE LORD (first wishing to you the grace of God, and all health and happiness), being informed that you bear a great delight, love, and affection to my writings, which hitherto have been unknown to you, I must answer you that the same likewise is a much greater delight and

surpassing joy in my spirit, because I understand that God does drive and carry on His work in such great and high persons, which is not a thing commonly to be found in the world, for the temporal honour and pleasure of this life is an hindrance to it.

2. But I can very well perceive in what manner God's Spirit has touched and awaked your noble heart, in token whereof you have bestowed so much pains and cost upon this work, which was written by a very simple and plain hand, without any art or great understanding, but only in the knowledge and manifestation of the gifts of God; and, moreover, it was not the intent of the author that it should come into the hands of so high persons, because he wrote it only for a memorandum to himself, to stir and rouse up himself from the dark and drowsy sleep in flesh and blood, and not out of an intention to make such a work.

3. Indeed there was a fiery instigation, but without foreknowledge of this work, that lay hid in him as a mystery, which the Spirit of God did stir up and awake; whereupon there arose a great longing and desire to write, and yet in respect of the outward man there was no desire, capacity, fitness, and ability in the author thereunto, for he sought only after the heart of God, to hide himself therein from the storm and raging tempest of the devil.

4. And he considered the evil nature and its working influences, and oftentimes the deceit of the devil, and the anger of God, and also the love and mercy of God, where, indeed, many a storm and strong encounter was held against reason, and also against flesh and blood and the devil, and all in a powerful driving and instigation of the spirit, till at last a most precious garland or diadem was set upon his head, which this hand cannot set down in writing; but I rather wish that the reader of this Epistle

great depth and full Chaos in the Mystery; yet without my sufficient comprehension, for the creature is not as God that does, and comprehends all things at once in His wisdom.

10. And there was then a purpose in me again to write something, and in the space of nine months three books were made, the one concerning the *Three Principles of the Divine Essence*; that is, of the Being of all beings, wherein the great mystery has somewhat opened and revealed itself, and therein are many excellent things contained much deeper than in this first work, viz., the *Aurora* (which your honour has sent hither for me to peruse), and it has about an hundred sheets of paper.

11. After this there was one made containing sixty sheets, which treats of the *Threefold Life of Man,* and also of the whole creation, a great open gate of the mystery, and 'tis even a wonder that surpasses and goes beyond the reach of all reason, at the which I myself in my reason do wonder and marvel what God intends to do; that He uses such a mean instrument to such weighty matters, for therein are revealed and laid forth the mysteries about which (since the heavy fall of Adam) the world has contended and always sought, yet there has not been such a ground brought to light which, notwithstanding, shall not be understood of the world, but of the children of God, as the same is manifest and known.

12. And then, Thirdly, there were *Forty Questions* sent to me of a learned and an understanding man who also is a lover of the mystery, and a great friend of the same, who exhorted me to answer them according to these gifts and spirit, which indeed are very high questions, and they contain in them the great depths and secrets of the original of the soul, and all the secrets or mysteries of the mystery,

whereupon there is such an answer brought forth, at which the world might well rejoice if the anger, iniquity, and malice of the devil did not hinder it, yet the counsel of God must stand.

13. Now because I perceive that your noble mind and heart has a singular hunger and thirst after such mysteries, and regard not the world which despises such mysteries; therefore I acknowledge the counsel of God herein, and it is my bounden duty to impart the same to you; for to the children belongs bread, they are worthy of it, but the pearl must not be cast before swine, for my spirit and mind shows me sufficiently that your honour searches not after such things out of curiosity, but from the instigation and guidance of the Spirit, which many times leads Peter to Cornelius, that he may tell and declare to him the words of eternal life.

14. And though I am a stranger, and very simple, yet your desire and will does embolden me to write to your honour, albeit in a plain and coarse style (but God's gifts are not bound to any human arts), and I am the more bold with you, because I perceive that your noble heart appears so low and humble as to send to me, who am but a mean and abject person; but seeing 'tis thus, I do likewise assuredly hope that the Spirit of God shall open the doors and gates of the mysteries for the soul, and grant a right understanding to apprehend and know His wonderful gifts, the which I heartily wish to your honour.

15. My writings will seem somewhat strange to you, for in some places the zeal is vehement or earnest, especially against Babel and the Antichrist, who is known by God in His anger; therefore I say that I could not, nor durst not, write otherwise than what was given to me. I have continually written as the Spirit did dictate it, and did not

give place to reason. I also do not acknowledge it for a work of my reason, which was too weak; but it is the work of the Spirit, who has shown what He means to do, and what shall come to pass, and also what is already done; for He proceeds forth out of the abyss into the byss, and searches through all things. He tries the heart and reins, and proves the thoughts of men; moreover, he does hereby intimate and declare the last Judgment; that He will try and examine every being through the fire; and I could not, neither might I write at all (even in the fiery instigation) except I did set it down as the Spirit did represent it; therefore I have made it for a memorandum to myself, I have no further intention therewith.

16. But because you are desirous to read the same, I will send it, and I pray you to return it back again, for I will keep it for a memorandum, and I am assured (that so far as your noble mind shall give God the praise, and read it diligently, and take this way to heart with a desire to understand the same) that the Lord will open to you the door of His love in the mystery, and crown you with the diadem of His wisdom, which is more precious than the created heaven and this world; for the precious philosopher's stone, the ground of all mysteries and secrets lies therein; and this same garland of wisdom is beset with this stone, which diadem and crown of light in the Holy Ghost the soul puts on as a garment, being a new body in, and for, the kingdom of God, wherein it is the child of God, and wherewith it is able to stand in the fire of God's anger without any hurt or grief, and can therein overcome the devil, death, and this world; and therein also can rule over the stars, the poisonous influences of the constellation, and this outward life, which otherwise is a thing impossible for reason; for it gives that knowledge of things which no art [or literal accruement from external

reason] is able to search out or dive into; it sees through heaven and earth, and it reaps where it has not sown; it asks not the question, *Is it true or no?* It has the sign of truth and righteousness in itself; it has all virtues lying in hope; there is no fear of God's anger in it; it affords a very joyful hope, and ratifies and assures the same; and it confirms the soul to be the child of God.

17. This garland is a virgin, and a chaste purity, and divine beauty; a joy of the life, it comforts and rejoices the mind in affliction, it goes along with man into death, but it has no death or dying in it; it lives from eternity, and it is a guide into heaven, and it is the joy of the angels; its taste is more precious and pleasant than all the joys of this world; and he that once obtains it, esteems it higher than all the goods and riches of this world; it cannot be paralleled but only with the Deity, but it lies hid in a dark valley; the world knows it not; the devil blows against it as a storm of wind, and does often so cover and disguise it that reason does not know it, but it springs forth in its time as a fair lily with manifold fruits; it is sown in tears, it grows in tribulation and affliction, but it is reaped with great joy; it is contemned and despised by reason, but he that obtains it holds it for his best treasure.

18. Such a garland is set upon him that seeks after it with earnestness, and wholly resigns up himself unto it, but not his self-reason in flesh and blood does obtain it, as my writings do fully testify; for what is therein written, the author has known by experience; there is no strange hand or spirit foisted in. I write not this for my own vain glory (my boasting is only in God), but for a rule and direction to the children of God, and that they may know what reward God gives to those who put their trust and confidence in Him, and regard not the dispraise and contempt of the world.

19. I do likewise wonder how you, and many more in Silesia, have gotten my writings, for I have no acquaintance with any of them; and I am so close in respect of publishing of them that the citizens here about me know nothing of them, save only of the first part, which was perforce taken from me; which by means of a person in the mystery of Babel (who persecuted it out of envy) was proclaimed among them for heresy; which notwithstanding they never read, neither was it examined ever as it was meet.

20. Indeed, I never asked any man's advice about it, or ever committed it to the censure and judgment of man to this very hour, but commended it to God; yet hereby I know and acknowledge the way of God; and likewise, I understand that it is known not only in Silesia, but also in other countries, without my foreknowledge; and I must even say, that he that has so persecuted it, he has thereby published it, for my intent was to keep it by me as long as I lived; and I wrote it for myself only.

21. But what God purposed in His counsel is now manifest, and it shall yet appear more clearly when the two last books (*The Three Principles* and *The Threefold Life*) shall be read, at the which I myself in the external man marvel and wonder what God intends, and will do; for I acknowledge myself to be altogether unworthy and ignorant, and yet the greatest and deepest mysteries are revealed to the internal man, which I give you and other lovers of God in humility to consider of; for in truth I cannot at all say that it is the work of my understanding or reason. But I acknowledge it to be a wonder, wherein God will reveal great things, whereinto my reason does speculate, and continually marvels at it.

22. For I never in all my life studied these mysteries, and likewise knew nothing of them, for I am a layman; and yet I must bring such things forth to light which all the high schools or universities have not been able to do; to whom notwithstanding in comparison I am but a child, and have none of their arts or wisdom, and I must write wholly from another school; and which is yet greater than all this, the language of Nature is made known to me, so that I can understand the greatest mysteries in my own mother's tongue.

23. Though I cannot say that I have learned or comprehended it, but as long as the hand of God stays upon me I understand it; but if it hides itself, then I know not my own labour, and am made a stranger to the work of my own hands; whereby I may see how altogether impossible a thing it is to search out and apprehend the mysteries of God without God's Spirit; therefore I ascribe and attribute nothing to myself; it is not my work, I desire not any human applause and honour for it.

24. I am only a simple, mean instrument, God works and makes what He pleases; what God wills, that I will also; and whatsoever He wills not, that likewise I will not; if it be His will for me to know anything, then I will know it; but if He wills it not, then do I so also. I will be nothing, and dead, that He may live and work in me what He pleases. I have cast myself wholly into Him, that so I may be safe and sure from the devil.

25. And though I must leave my outward body and life to the disposal of the world, and suffer the devil to roar against me, yet I will not trust neither the devil nor the world with my internal man; neither will I do (according to the inward man) what the world will have me; and albeit my outward man is bound and obliged to the world,

and in its obligation and allegiance must obey the laws and ordinances of the world, and do what the outward obligation requires of me, yet my internal man shall only be obedient to God, and not to the world; for he is not in the world, but has made himself dead thereto, that God might live in him, and be both the will and the deed in him; and though I cannot say that it is possible to live in perfection, yet my will is so directed and bent; and this neither the world nor the devil shall break, albeit my outward life should faint and perish, and though reason does oftentimes flatly gainsay it, and temptation appears by heaps, to the terror and sadness of the external life (where the spirit also hides itself, as if all were dead and gone), yet it brings forth always new fruits, and that in abundance.

26. This I have related to you at large, that you may know and acknowledge what manner of man I am, and what the beginning and cause of my writing is, and from what art and spirit it was produced or generated; and also to what end—namely, to keep it as a memorandum to myself; but because I perceive honest religious hearts to thirst after it, therefore I will not conceal it from them but impart, in a brotherly and Christian way, and commend and commit it to God, that He may work and do what He pleases in them; and this we are bound and obliged to do one for another.

27. Lastly, I entreat you to conceal my name among the learned, for I know that a mean layman is accounted but ridiculous and contemptible with men learned in scholastic art; and though God has His children also among them, yet I care not for having my name put upon it, or authorised upon me; for the praise belongs to God, who is the giver. I do not seek to make myself thereby a great and glorious name; but Christ is my reward, my

name and glory, and I hope to have the glory of it in the life to come before angels and men, and to rejoice therein with the saints in Christ, as my writings sufficiently testify.

28. Concerning the book *Aurora*, which your honour has sent me to peruse, I have read some of it over, and find that it is my work, and well copied out; but some syllables are left out for brevity sake, and yet the sense and meaning is not thereby diminished; I am well contented for all that, seeing (so far as I have perused in haste) I have found no addition, but the great mysteries are couched therein very deep; they were understood and apprehended by the author, but it was not very feasible for reason to comprehend it at the first time, although it was known in the depth well enough, yet the author was not accustomed to it; when the heavenly joy met him, then he only followed the Spirit's guidance, but the wild nature is not presently regenerated [or made a new creature]. Indeed, if a kernel be sown there grows a tree; but if the virtue be great [if the power of the resolution be strong, and the practice sincere and constant] the tree grows up the sooner, and is the sooner known.

29. In the other three books you shall find the mysteries more clearly, and so throughout, the further the deeper; each book from the first is grounded ten times deeper; so that the fourth is a very clear mirror, wherein the great mystery is sufficiently and visibly seen and understood, yet only by its children; reason shall remain blind, for the Spirit of God dwells not in the outward principle, but in the inward; and proceeds forth from the inward into the outward principle of this world, yet the outward does not comprehend him.

30. But, sir, I must tell you that the book *Aurora* was not finished, for the devil intended to make a bonfire of it, because he saw that the day would break forth in it; but for all that, the day has even overtaken the *Aurora*, so that it is already clear day; there belong yet about thirty sheets to it; but because the storm did break them off, it was not finished; and in the meantime it is grown daylight, and the morning is extinguished; and since that time the labour has been to bring forth the day: yet it shall remain so for an eternal remembrance, because the defect is restored, and supplied in the second (the book of the *Three Principles*); the fault and blame of the defect is to be attributed to the enemy.

31. But I will lay the fault upon none, but only the falsehood and iniquity of the devil, who is an enemy to all good, who even confounds and entangles kings. How shall a poor mean man, being employed in such a work, be acknowledged and known? If it is affirmed that he is an unlearned layman, the very wise and skillful in arts will be offended at his plainness and simplicity. When he hears one speak of such wonders and deep mysteries in such a mean and simple way, without scholastic pomp of words and artificial terms, and phrases of logic and rhetoric, then he thinks it is a rhapsody, for he understands not the gifts of God, and also is not able to see into the heart of another; therefore I will disturb no man, and desire none to trouble himself about it; but I confess that it is God's providence, else this book should have yet lain in a corner.

32. But thus it was published without my knowledge, consent, and will, and that by the persecutors themselves, the which I acknowledge to be from the providence and appointment of God; for I had no copy of it for myself; neither did I ever know those that have it, also I have it

not myself, and yet it has been copied out; and brought to my sight and hands four times already; so that I see that others have published it; and I esteem it a wonderful work, that the grain grows against the will of the enemy: but that which is sown by God, none can hinder.

33. But that which you and others also do misconstrue in my book Aurora (which appears to be wrong in the apprehension, and which also needs some clearing and exposition), you shall find sufficiently cleared at large in my third and fourth book; wherein there is an open gate of the mysteries of all beings; and there is even nothing in nature, but it might be fundamentally searched out, and grounded upon this way; for it shows and opens the stone of the wise men unto all the secrets and mysteries both in the divine and earthly mystery—by this knowledge, and understanding, all the metals of the earth may be brought to the highest degree of perfection, yet only by the children of the divine *magia*, who have the same revelation.

34. I see it well enough, but I have no manual operation, instigation or art unto it; but I only set forth an open mystery, whereunto God shall stir up labourers of His own; let no man seek the work from me, or think to get the knowledge and operation of the philosopher's stone (or universal tincture) from me, and though it is known clearly, and might be opened more clearly, yet I have broken my will, and will write nothing, but as it is given to me, that so it may not be my work, lest I should be imprisoned in the *Turba*.

35. And if you will have anything copied out of these writings now sent to you, it is requisite that the transcriber be a learned, understanding man; for many syllables are not fully written, neither have all grammatical

autography, and in many words some letters may be wanting, and sometimes a capital letter stands for a whole word, for art has not written here, neither was there any time to consider how to set it down punctually according to the right understanding of the letters, but all was ordered according to the direction of the Spirit which often went in haste, so that the penman's hand (by reason that he was not accustomed to it) did often shake; and though I could have written in a more accurate, fair, and plain manner; yet the reason was this, that the burning fire did often force forward with speed, and the hand and pen must hasten directly after it; for it cometh and goes as a sudden shower, whatsoever it lights upon it hits; if it were possible to comprehend and write all that my mind beholds in the divine CHAOS, it would then be three times more, and deeper grounded.

36. But it cannot be, and therefore there is more than one book made; more than one philosophical discourse, and throughout deeper, so that what could not be contained in the one might be found in the other, and it were well that at last, out of all, only one might be made and all the others laid aside, for the multiplicity and plurality causes strife, contrariety, averseness, and wrong apprehensions by reason of the sudden catching conceits, and conjectures of the reader, which knows not to try and discern the Spirit, which uses such wonderful phrase, where oftentimes reason supposes that it contradicts itself; and yet in the depth it is not contrary at all.

37. Out of which misunderstanding [or feigned glosses of reason and literal outward art upon the writings of holy men] the great Babel upon earth has been brought forth, where men contend for nothing but words; but let the spirit of understanding in the mystery alone, but its end and number is found and committed to the *Turba*; for the

beginning has found the limit, and there is no more any withholding of the wrath of God upon Babel; it cannot be quashed by any power or force of arms.

38. I speak not of and from myself, but from that which the Spirit shows, which no man can resist; for it stands in its omnipotence, and depends not on our thinking and willing, as the fourth book (*the Forty Questions*) of these writings does exceeding deeply declare, which is strongly grounded in the light of nature, and can be demonstrated in all things.

39. Further, I give you to understand that in these writings which are now sent you, the author uses sometimes to speak of himself, *we*, and sometimes *I*. Now understand by the word *we*, the spirit (being spoken in the plural) in two persons; and in the word *I*, the author understands himself; this I give you for direction and information, to take away wrong apprehension and suspicion.

40. And herewith I send you the fourth part, being *the Forty Questions,* and therein you may behold yourself, and at the next opportunity I will send you the second and third parts, if you desire to have them; and I pray to return it to me again by the next occasion, for I will send it to him who framed and sent me the questions; and so I commend and commit you to the love of God, heartily wishing that God would illuminate your noble heart, and give you rightly to understand the sense and meaning of the author in the internal principle, with all temporal and eternal welfare.

Yours in the love of J. C.,

J. B.,

Teutonicus. Dated, Gorlitz, 1620.

AURORA Chapter 19
Concerning *Heaven.*

1. THE true heaven, which is our own proper human heaven, into which the soul goes when it departs from the body, and into which Christ our King has entered, and from whence it was that he came from his Father, and was born, and became man in the body or womb of the Virgin Mary, has hitherto been hidden from the children of men, and they have had many opinions about it.

2. Also the learned have scuffled about it with many strange scurrilous writings, falling upon one another in calumnious and disgraceful terms, whereby the holy name of God has been reproached, his members wounded, his temple destroyed, and the holy heaven profaned with their calumniating and malicious enmity.

3. Men have always been of the opinion that heaven is many hundred, nay, many thousand miles distant from the face of the earth, and that God dwells only in that heaven.

4. Some naturalists have undertaken to measure that height and distance, and have invented many strange and monstrous devices. Before I knew that which I deeply know now, I, like others, thought that there was no other true heaven than that which as a blue circle encloses the world high above the stars; thinking that God had a separate existence therein, and that He was ruling this world by means of His Holy Spirit.

5. But after I had met with many a hard obstacle in following out this theory, I fell into a state of deep melancholy and heavy sadness in beholding the great depth of this world, the sun and the stars, the clouds, rain and snow, and in fact the whole of creation. I compared

all that with the little speck called man and how insignificant he is before God, if compared with this great work of heaven and earth,

6. Wherein then I found to be in all things, evil and good, love and anger, in the inanimate creatures, viz. in wood, stones, earth and the elements, as also in men and beasts.

7. Moreover, I considered the little spark of light, man, why he should have any value for God, in comparison with this great firmament of heaven and earth.

8. But finding that in all things there was evil and good, in the elements and in the creatures, and that it went as well in this world with the wicked as with the virtuous; also that the barbarous people had the best lands in their possession, and that they had more prosperity in their ways than the virtuous, honest and Godly had.

9. I was thus very melancholy, perplexed and exceedingly troubled, no Scripture could comfort or satisfy me, though I was very well acquainted with it; at which time the devil by no means stood idle, but was often beating into me many heathenish thoughts, which I will not mention here.

10. But when in this affliction and trouble I earnestly raised my spirit up into God, as with a great storm or onslaught, wrapping up my whole heart and mind, thoughts, will and resolution, incessantly to wrestle with the love and mercy of God, and not to give over, until he blessed me (Genesis 32:24-26), that is, until he enlightened me with his Holy Spirit, whereby I might understand his will, and be rid of my sadness. *And then the spirit broke through.*

11. For in my resolved zeal, I gave so hard an assault, storm and onslaught upon God, and upon all the gates of

hell, with a resolution to hazard my life upon it (which assuredly was not in my ability without the assistance of the spirit of God), suddenly, after some violent storms, my spirit broke through the gates of hell, even into the innermost birth of the Deity, and there I was embraced with love, as a bridegroom embraces his dearly beloved bride.

12. But the greatness of the triumphing that was in the spirit I cannot express, either in speaking or writing; neither can it be compared to anything, but to life is generated in the midst of death, and it is like the resurrection from the dead.

13. In this light my spirit suddenly saw through all, and in and by all the creatures, even in herbs and grass it knew God, who he is, and how he is, and what his will is: And suddenly in that light my will was set on by a mighty impulse, to describe the being of God.

14. But because I could not at once apprehend the deepest births of God in their being, and comprehend them in my reason, there passed almost twelve years, before the exact understanding was given me.

15. It was with me as with a young tree that is planted in the ground, and at first is young and tender, and flourishing to the eye, especially if it comes on lustily in its growing: But it does not bear fruit at once; and though it blossoms, the blossoms fall off; also many a cold wind, frost and snow pass over it, before it comes to any growth and bearing of fruit.

16. So also it went with this spirit: The first fire was but a seed, and not a constant lasting light: Since that time many a cold wind blew upon it; but the will never was extinguished.

16a. This tree was also often tempted to try whether it would bear fruit, and show itself with blossoms; but the blossoms were struck off till this very time, wherein it stands in its first fruit, in the growth or vegetation.

17. From this light now it is that I have my knowledge, as also my will, impulse and driving, and therefore I will set down this knowledge in writing according to my gift, and let God work his will; and though I should irritate or enrage the whole world, the devil, and all the gates of hell, I will look on and wait what the LORD intends with it.

18. For I am much too weak to know his purpose; and though the Spirit grants in the light to be known some things which are to come, yet according to the outward man I am too weak to comprehend it all.

19. But the animated or soulish spirit, which qualifies or unites with God, that comprehends it well; but the bestial body attains only a glimpse thereof, just as if lightning flashed: For thus presents itself the innermost birth or geniture of the soul, when it tears through the outermost birth or geniture in the elevation of the Holy Ghost, and so breaks through the gates of hell; but the outermost birth presently shuts again; for the wrath of God bolts up the firmament, and holds it captive in its power.

20. Then the knowledge of the outward man is gone, and he walks up and down in an afflicted and anxious birth or geniture, as a woman with child, who is in her travail, and would always fain bring forth her child, but cannot, and is full of throes.

21. Thus it goes also with the bestial body, when it has once tasted of the sweetness of God, then it continually hungers and thirsts after this sweetness: But the devil in

the power of God's wrath opposes exceedingly, and so a man in such a course must continually stand in an anxious birth or geniture; and so there is nothing but fighting and warring in his births or genitures.

22. I write this not for mine own glory, but for the comfort of the Reader, so that if perhaps you are minded to walk with me upon my narrow bridge, you will not suddenly be discouraged, dismayed and distrustful, when the gates of hell and God's wrath meet you, and present themselves before you.

23. When we pass together over this narrow bridge of the fleshly birth, to yonder green meadow, where the wrath of God does not reach, then we shall greatly rejoice at all the damages and hurts which we have sustained; though indeed at present the world accounts us fools, and we must suffer the devil in the power of God's wrath to domineer, and to rush and roar over us: It should not trouble us, for it will be a more excellent reputation to us in the other life, than if in this life we had worn a royal crown; and there is so very short a time to get there, that it is not worth being called "a time." Now observe:

24. If you fix your thoughts concerning heaven, and wish to conceive in the mind what it is, and where it is, and how it is, you need not to swing or cast your thoughts many thousand miles off, for that place, or that heaven, is not your heaven.

26. For the true heaven is everywhere.

54. If man's eyes were but opened, he would see God everywhere in his heaven; for heaven stands in the innermost birth or geniture everywhere.

55. Moreover, when Stephen saw the heaven opened, and the Lord JESUS at the right hand of God, there his spirit did not first swing itself up aloft into the upper heaven, but it penetrated or pressed into the innermost birth or geniture, wherein heaven is everywhere.

56. Neither must thou think that the Deity is such a kind of being as is only in the upper heaven, nor that the soul, when it departs from the body, goes up aloft into the upper heaven many hundred thousand miles off.

57. It need not do that, but it is set or put into the innermost birth, and there it is with God, and in God, and with all the holy angels, and can now be above, and now beneath; it is not hindered by anything.

58. For in the innermost birth the upper and nether Deity is one body, and is an open gate: The holy angels converse and walk up and down in the innermost birth of this world by and with our King JESUS CHRIST, as well as in the uppermost world aloft in their quarters, courts or region.

59. And where then would or should the soul of man rather be, than with its King and Redeemer JESUS CHRIST? For near and far off in God is one thing, one comprehensibility, Father, Son and Holy Ghost, everywhere all over.

60. The gate of the Deity in the upper heaven is no other, also no brighter, than it is in this world: And where can there be greater joy than in that place, where every hour and moment there cometh to Christ beautiful, loving, dear, newborn children and angels, who are pressed or penetrated through death into life?

61. Doubtless they will have to tell of many fights: and where can there be greater joy, than where, in the midst or centre of death, life is generated continually?

62. Does not every soul bring along with it a new triumph? and so there is nothing else but an exceeding friendly welcoming and salutation there.

From EPISTLE 1
29. We are taught, indeed, an imputed grace, but what faith is and how it is begotten, and what it is in its essence, real being, and substance, and how it lays hold on the merit of Christ with the grace; herein the greatest part are dumb and blind, and depend on an historical faith (James 2) which is only a bare knowledge or literal conjecture, and with it the man of sin tickles and comforts himself, and through a vain imagination and blind persuasion, flatters and soothes himself, and calls himself a Christian, though he is not yet become either capable or worthy of this so high a title, but is a Christian in name only, externally clothed with Christ's purple mantle, of whom the prophet speaks, saying: They draw near to Me with their lips, but their heart is far from Me; and Christ said: Not all that say Lord, Lord, shall enter into the kingdom of heaven, but they that do the will of My Father in heaven.

30. Now Christ alone is the will of the Father, in whom the acceptance of grace and adoption consists, and none can do the love-will of the Father, except that only Throne of Grace, Christ himself, as the holy Scripture declares, no man can call God Lord, without the holy Spirit in him. (1 Corinthians 12:3)

31. For we know not what and how to pray before God as we ought, but He, the Holy Spirit in Christ, makes intercession for us, with unutterable sighs before God in ourselves, as it pleases God; we cannot attain anything by our willing and knowing; He is too deeply hidden from us, for it lies not in any man's knowing, willing, running, and searching, but in God's mercy.

32. Now there is no mercy but only in Christ, and if I shall reach that mercy, then I must reach Christ in me; are my sins to be destroyed in me? Then must Christ do it in me with His blood and death, with His victory over hell: Am I to believe? then must the Spirit, desire, and will of Christ believe in my desire and will, for I cannot believe.

33. But He receives my will being resigned to Him, and comprehends it in His own will, and brings it through His victory into God, and there He intercedes for the will of my soul in His own will before God, and so I am received as a child of grace in His will of love.

34. For the Father has manifested his love in Christ, and Christ manifests that same love in my will, surrendered to Him; Christ draws my will into Himself, and clothes it with His blood and death, and tinctures it with the highest tincture of the divine power, and so it is changed into an angelical image, and gets a divine life.

FROM *APOLOGIA: BALTHAZAR TILCKEN*

20. Surely, were I to write concerning myself as if I were a Great Master of the Scriptures or Arts and Sciences of the Schools or Universities of this World, that is NOT so; I am a poor simple Man, and have my Skill and high knowledge, not from Art or from Reason, neither have I sought for Great Art, but from my Youth up have sought

only the Salvation of my Soul, how I might inherit and possess the Kingdom of God.

21. But after I found in me a powerful Opposition, viz., the driving in Flesh and Blood, and the mighty strife between the Woman's and the Serpent's Seed, I then once set myself so hard in strife against the Serpent's Seed, and my own corrupt Nature, yet through the assistance of God, that I supposed I should overcome and break that innate evil Will and Inclination, and unite myself to the Love of God in Christ, to hide myself in the Heart or Bosom of God, from the terrible Tempest of the Anger of God, and the fierce wrath of the Devil, that, God's Spirit might rule, drive and lead me.

22. I purposed to keep myself as dead in my innate form and Condition, till the Spirit got a Form in me, and that I laid hold of him, that I might lead my Life through and in him.

23. Also I purposed to Will nothing, but what I apprehended in his Will and Light; he should be my Will and Deed: which indeed was not possible for me to Do, and yet I stood in the Earnest purpose and resolution, and in very earnest strife and Battle against myself.

8. But if the devil should raise mockers and despisers, who would say it doth not become me to climb so high into the Deity, and to dive so deeply thereinto:

9. To all of them I give this for an answer. That I am not climbed up into the Deity, neither is it possible for such a mean man as I am to do it; but the Deity is climbed up into me, and from its love are these things revealed to me, which otherwise I, in my half-dead fleshly birth or geniture, must needs have let alone altogether.

III. ANTICHRIST

THE THREEFOLD LIFE OF MAN chapter 11

The Great Open Gate of the Antichrist

51 Hearken and see, you poor soul, we will show you the very Antichrist who domineers over the whole world, whom God has made known to us that you might see him: for you have hitherto accounted him a god; but now his shame must come to light: for he is so secret that none know him, unless they are born of God, so that they apprehend God's essence and will, otherwise he remains hidden in every man; for there is none who does not have him, and carry him in his heart; yea, if one is a child of God, and yet has not the deep knowledge of God, he still hangs to him: for the devil has insinuated himself in the form of an angel into him: Therefore mark what here follows, for it is the number of the Seventh Seal, and declares the eternal day.

52. Observe it, ye children of God, for I myself formerly, before the time of my high knowledge, did thus reverence and honour him, and supposed it was according to God's will: for I was taught no otherwise; and the whole world is in the same conceit. For here the devil will lose his sting in the children of God, into whose hearts this knowledge shall spring up: for it is the right steel wherewith God's love-fire is struck, and whereby the soul receives Christ's body, and is born in God: for the soul needs no other birth, but a returning and entering into God.

53. Behold! you poor wounded soul, you stand and pray thus, O God, forgive me my sins, let your anger cease, and receive me into your grace; and it is very well done; but you do not understand how God receives a poor

sinner: You suppose it is as when you come before the prince or judge of the land, and have forfeited your life, and plead for mercy, and he of grace forgives your misdeed, and so you are freed: But your sins fly in your face, and your heart accuses you, that you art yet guilty of the punishment: And just thus you come also before God: and so many hypocrites are thereby generated: You suppose God, in his essence and spirit, takes your sins away from you: Do you not know what the Scripture says, that all our works shall follow us? And if it shall happen, as aforesaid, then God must move himself upon everyone's will and purpose to call upon him, and cast away his sins from him, and yet from eternity God has moved himself no more but twice; once with the creation of the world and all creatures; and a second time in Christ's becoming man, and there the Heart of God moved itself. [Note: The third time God will move himself in the power of the Holy Ghost through the mouth of Christ at the Last Judgment Day, when all shall return again into the ether: The first moving is according to the Father; the second according to the Son; and the third according to the Holy Ghost; otherwise he moves himself no more in eternity.]

54. Behold! when God forgives you your sins, when you call upon him, he takes nothing away from you, neither does he fly down from heaven into you, for he is from eternity in your soul, but in his own Principle; your soul, as to him, is only gone out from his Principle; understand, out from the holy will in the Majesty, into the anger. Now, in the anger, you were in the eternal death, and the man Christ, who is God and man, has made a passage through the death and anger to the Majesty of God; you need only to turn, and go through that passage, through the death of Christ, through the anger into the Majesty,

and so you will be embraced as the most beloved angel, that never committed any sin: also no sin will be known in you, but God's deeds of wonder only, which must be opened in the anger: for the love has nothing to do with that fire, [viz. the love cannot open the wonders of the anger], neither does it mix itself with the fire of wrath, but flies from it.

55. Now, therefore, when you pray thus, *O God! forgive me*; you always doubt, because of your sins, whether God will hear you, and come into your heart. Behold! do not doubt; for by your doubting you despise and contemn the Majesty: It is also a sin; but cast all your sins in general upon a heap, and come confidently with your desiring soul, in humility, to God, and enter into him: Turn your soul out from the will of this world into the will of God: cast yourself, with your whole reason, and all your thoughts, into the will of God; and although your heart and the devil say, No, yet make your outward reason dead, and enter in with force, and continue steadfast: Look not back, as Lot's wife did, who was turned again into sulphur, and into a pillar of salt, but stand fast: Let the devil, and the spirit of this world, and also your heart, with flesh and blood, struggle, yet give no place to reason; when it says, You art outside of God, then say, No, I am in God, I am in heaven in him, I will not in eternity depart from him: The devil may keep my sins, and the world this body, yet I live in the will of God; his life shall be also my life, and his will shall be my will: I will be dead as to my reason, that HE may live in me: All my doing shall be his doing: Give yourself up to him, in all your purposes: Whatsoever you take in hand, commit it to his pleasure and government, that all may be done in his will: Behold! if you do thus, all evil lusts will depart from you; for you stand fast in the presence of God, and the Virgin of his

wisdom leads you, and opens to you the way to eternal life, she warns you of the evil or false ways, she always drives you on to abstinence or amendment, and submission or resignation.

56. But, that you have so great obstacles and hindrances of doubting in this way, is caused by the strife of the soul against the devil, who lays himself in the way as a filthy swine; therefore cast your sins upon his neck, and do not doubt; and if you cannot leave that [doubting], then reach with your soul into God, for God is in you: Christ has opened the gates into his Father; do but enter in, let nothing keep you back; and though heaven and earth, and all the creatures, should say you canst not, believe them not, go forward, and you wilt suddenly get in; and as soon as you come in, you get a new body on to the soul, that is, the body of Christ, which is God and man; and you wilt afterwards have ease and refreshment in your heart; you will get one that will draw you, and set the falsehood of the world before your eyes, and warn you of it.

57. Therefore, observe, there are many that think with themselves, saying, I will pray to God to take away my sins from me, that I may be released of my old sins: and when it comes to pass that they attain the love of God, they think the old sins are passed away and forgiven; saying, I may now sin anew, I will afterwards repent once again, and cast the abomination away from me: Indeed that would be a good way, if the purpose were at hand: But hear, when you go out from the love of God, then you have all your sins, which you hast committed all your life long, upon your neck again: for you turn back again into the house of sin, and forsake God; you go out from God into the kingdom of the devil, and your works follow you

whithersoever you go: The purpose cannot help you, unless you go on in your purpose.

58. Or do we alone say this? Does not Christ say, When the unclean spirit goes out from a man, he walks through dry places, seeking rest and finding none; and then he returns again into his house, and when he coms there, he finds it swept and trimmed; and then he goes and takes with him seven other spirits, which are worse than himself, and enters in, and dwells there, and so the last [condition] of that man is worse than the first? Do you understand this similitude? You have driven out Satan, and have cleansed your heart, and have well swept your house of sin, and trimmed it; and now, when you are secure and careless, then comes the devil with all the seven forms of nature, and slips in, and thrusts the old worldly lusts into your heart again, out of which all wickedness and blasphemies are generated; for he dwells in those seven spirits, and tickles your heart therewith, and deceives you seven times more, and so you yield to him, and fall from one sin into another; and then he binds the poor soul fast to the sin, and lets it not run after abstinence or amendment, but brings it into fleshly lusts; and when the soul begins to stir, he says, *Tomorrow, tomorrow*: so long till he get the venison.

59. Therefore it is said, *We must stand still and watch; for the devil goes about as a roaring lion, seeking whom he may devour*: He comes at all hours before the door of your heart, to see whether he can get in or no: for it is his beloved lodging: He has no rest in hell, but in the soul of man he has joy and pleasure: he can therein open his malicious wonders, wherewith he may sport himself after this time also, wherein he takes his pleasure; for hell and the anger of God desires that.

60. Again, you see how the great whore of Babel has set herself up in her play of forgiving sins: She boasts of the keys of Absolution, that she can forgive sins, and boasts of the Apostolical Keys, and makes sale of sins for money, and usurps that from Christ's words, Whose sins ye remit, &c. [John 20:23]

61. Now I would fain know, how the sins of the repentant sinner, who casts himself into God's will, and who goes forth from this world's reason into God's mercy, can have his sins retained? And much more would I fain know, how one sinful man can fetch another out of hell into the kingdom of heaven, when he cannot get in himself, and goes about only to make the devil proud with his covetousness, in that he sells the forgiveness of sins for money? Whereas all sins are drowned only in Christ's New Body, in Christ's flesh and blood: And Isaiah says, in the person of Christ, I tread the winepress alone: and I alone blot out your sins, and none besides me. But if it were true, which Antichrist boasts of, then one devil must drive away another; and then, what would become of the New Regeneration in Christ's flesh and blood, whereby our souls are brought into God?

62. If it could possibly have been that God might have taken away Adam's sin in such a manner, God needed not to become man, and so have brought us into God again: He might rather have forgiven Adam his sin, as a prince pardons a murderer, and grants him his life: No, you yourself must go out from sin, and enter into the will of God; for God does not stand by as a king, and forgive sins with words: It must be power: You must go out from the fire into the light; for God is no image for us to stand before, and give good words to, but he is a Spirit, and penetrates through the heart and reins, that is, soul and spirit: He is the fire of love, and his centre of nature is the

fire of anger; and if you were in hell among all the devils, yet then you are in God, for the anger is also his, it is his abyss; and therefore when you go out from that, you go into the love of God, into the liberty that is without pain.

63. There is no other forgiveness of sins, but that you go out from the will of this world, and of your flesh also, from the devil's will, into God's will; and then God's will receives you, and so you are freed from all sins, for they remain in the fire, and your will remains in the tincture of God, which the Majesty enlightens: All is near you; your sins are near you, but they touch you not; for, as we have mentioned to you before, the still eternity is a liberty; but yet do not think that it will take away your sins from you into itself, as also your abominations and wickedness; but they belong to the anger of God, there they must swim, and be bestowed on the devil; but they stand beneath you in the centre, and you art as a fair sprout which springs up forth through the anger, to the love-fire, and to God's deeds of wonder; and yet the anger is not in God, but in the abyss; and when the devil lifted himself above God, then he went into the abyss, and became God's footstool.

64. The text in Matthew 16: 18-19, has another understanding in it: The Temple of Christ (viz. Christ's children) is Christ's Bride, he has adorned her with his fairest ornament; and, as he has loved us, and brought us through himself into God, his Father, so we should love one another:

The Gate of IMMANUEL.

82. Behold, dear soul, how faithfully Christ warns us concerning these times, concerning which we have been hitherto blind: For these false self-erected priests will cry out and say, *Christ is in the wilderness*: Another of them will say, *He is not in the wilderness, he is in the chamber,*

or he is in the field; and another again will say, *No, he is here or there, or he is in the Supper, or in the Baptism*; and another will say, *He is not in them, they are only signs and symbols*: But Christ says, *Believe them not, and go not forth; for as the lightning shines from the east to the west, so also shall the coming of the Son of Man be; for where the carcass is, thither the eagles gather together.* (Matthew 24:26-28)

83. Christ says, *I am the Way, the Truth, and the Life, none cometh to the Father, but by me: I am the Door to the Sheepfold, and am a Good Shepherd; but all that came before me, in their own name, of themselves, are thieves and murderers, and seek only to rob and steal; for they seek their own honour, but I seek not my own honour, but my Father honours me, and they dishonour me: I am the Light of the World, whosoever follows me, shall have the light of the eternal life; my Father will give the Holy Ghost to them that pray unto him for it; when he shall come, he shall lead you into all truth, for he shall receive of mine, and make it known unto you: Take no care of your life, for my Father cares for you: for where your heart is, there is your treasure also.*

84. Which is as much as to say: Run not after the self-erected teachers, who teach from the history, without the spirit of God: If they can speak a little in a strange language, then they will be teachers, and teach out of art and vainglory, to exercise their eloquence, wherein one flattering hypocrite helps forward the other, especially where much money and honour may be gotten in the office. Christ said, *I seek not my own honour; my kingdom is not of this world*: But they teach that Christ's kingdom is in the history, (viz. in learning, in eloquence, in the universities, in synods and councils). But Christ said to his disciples, *The Holy Ghost will receive of mine, and*

make it known unto you, and bring into your mind all whatsoever I have spoken.

85. Turn away your heart and mind from all contention, and go in very simply and humbly at the door of Christ, into Christ's sheepfold; seek that in your heart; you need not much disputation: Pray to God the Father, in the name of Jesus Christ, upon his promise, that he would open your heart through his holy spirit, turn with all diligence into him, let all go whatsoever makes a fine glistering holy show in the heaps of stone, and enter into the temple of Christ, and there the Holy Ghost will meet you: Yield yourself entirely up unto him, and he will open your heart, and bring into your mind all the merits and benefits of Christ; he will open your understanding, and bring into your mind whatsoever Christ has spoken, for he shall receive from Christ, and make it known unto you.

86. Neither trouble yourself with taking care where the best place is for him to open it in, (whether in a retreat, a college, a wilderness; in this or that office, ministry, or opinion) for, as the sun rises in the east, and shines to the west, so Christ shines in every corner and chink of his Incarnation, or *being man*, even to eternity: seek not after one place more than after another, he is everywhere; for where the carcass is, thither the eagles gather together: Christ is everywhere, and his children can come to him everywhere, and when we enter into Christ, then we are with our carcass, and satiate ourselves with his flesh, and drink of his blood; for he said, *My flesh is the true food, and my blood is the true drink, they that eat of my flesh and drink of my blood continue in Me, and I in them.* Also, he says, *Father, I will that those whom thou hast given me, may be where I am; they were thine, and thou hast given them unto me, and I give them the eternal life;*

and I will raise them up at the Last Day: if you continue in me, then my words continue in you.

95. But the Antichristian kingdom lives in many trees; they run from one to another, and know not which is the best, for they are gone forth from the paradise of Christ; they boast of the doctrine of Christ, and deny the power thereof, and thereby they testify that Christ is not in them: nay, they desire not to have him in them: they thrust him, with his body and blood, with his humanity, out of the congregation, they will have a sign from him, whereby they may in their pride possess his place, and so keep up their rich fat bellies: Christ, in this outward life upon earth, was poor, and had not whereon to lay his head: But they in Christ's place will be rich and fat: they say, He is in heaven, we will therefore erect a stately glorious pompous kingdom to his honour, that we may enjoy good times, and honour in his office. We are the highest in this world, for we are God's stewards, we manage the office of Christ, and have the *Mysterium Magnum*: How dare any speak against us? We will quickly make them hold their peace.

96. O beloved children of Christ, open your eyes, and see; do not run so after the devil; do you not see? Pray learn to see! Do you not see how all is done for money? If one give them store of money, they praise him for a gracious Christian, who is beneficial and bountiful to the Church: If one die, though all his life long he was an unjust false usurer, whoremonger, thief, and murderer, and they knew it very well, if he or his bestow much upon the Church [colleges or learned men], O how is he applauded for a blessed and glorious man! What great sermons do they make for him, that other unrighteous men may hear and consider, and follow their example to do the like? But stay, does the kingdom of Christ consist in such [giving

of] money, and in the mouth of the priest? No, it shall not prosper; here the winepress yieldeth much blood, as the Revelation of John speaketh.

THE TENTH EPISTLE.
Of the Killing of Antichrist in Ourselves.
Our Salvation is in Christ Jesus.

1. WORTHY and much respected sir, I wish unto you the grace, knowledge, and blessing of God in Christ Jesus; after I was informed of D. K. that you as a Christian brother, and fellow-member in the Lord, do stand in a hearty desire in the drawing of the Father to Christ Jesus; and do also labour in your mind how you may come to divine contemplation and vision in yourself; therefore upon the request of the doctor, I would not omit to visit and salute you with a short epistle, and briefly to declare unto you out of my gifts, out of Christian love, the way to divine vision and feeling; and hereby to present unto you in brotherly love the sap of my little coral in the spirit and life of Jesus Christ, as one branch or twig on the tree is bound to do to the other; and I desire that I might be well understood, if peradventure I might give further occasion to your zeal.

2. Seeing that you very well perceive in yourself that Antichrist in Babel rules in Christendom, and acts in selfhood and the lust of the flesh; and that our dear Immanuel has faithfully warned us of this, and said that flesh and blood shall not inherit the kingdom of Heaven (John vi.). And yet the Antichrist seeks and desires nothing else, but only temporal honour, might, and power, to climb up and advance himself in the lust of the flesh; and, moreover, that this Antichrist has for a long time so

civilly and demurely decked and adorned himself with Christ's purple mantle and His seamless coat, that men have not discerned him, but they have honoured and adored him for a saint; which is reasonably well revealed to me in the grace of the Most High; and thereupon I would declare unto you in brief what a Christian is, and also what the Antichrist in man is, for your further consideration.

3. Christ says: *Whosoever will not forsake houses, land, money, goods, wife, children, brothers and sisters, and deny himself and follow Me, is not My disciple*; also, *you must turn and become like children, or be born anew of water and the spirit, else you shall not see the kingdom of God.* This is not meant that one should run out of his vocation and calling, and from his wife and children into a solitary desert and wilderness, and forsake all; but only he must forsake the Antichrist, that is, the SELF in all [the *meum* and *tuum*, the mine and thine].

4. Whosoever will attain to divine contemplation and feeling within himself, he must mortify the Antichrist in his soul, and depart from all ownhood of the will; yea, from all creatures, and become the poorest creature in the ownhood [selfness or self-interest] of his mind, so that he has or owneth nothing any more for a propriety, be he in what estate and condition he will.

5. And though he be a king yet his mind must forsake all ownhood, and esteem himself in his place, dignity, and temporal goods no other than a servant of God; and that he therein ought to serve God and his brethren, and that he has and possesses all that he has, not after the right of nature, as if it were his own [to do according to his own will and pleasure therein], but that it is his fellow-brethren's and members'; and that God has set him as a

steward and officer over it; and he must think that he therein serves his Lord, who will require an account of him.

6. He must wholly and fully resign up in himself his own will (which drives him to such possession of ownhood [or selfish affection or union with the creature]) to the suffering and dying in the death of Jesus Christ; and humbly beseech God, in right earnest repentance and conversion, that He would mortify this evil will to selfness and temporal lust, in the death of Jesus Christ, and bring the will of his soul into the true adoption or filiation of God, that so he might not will and desire any longer to his self, but that God's will might be in him his will and desire; that he might be dead (as to the will of the soul) in and to his self or ownhood, and that God in Christ might be his life.

7. He must wholly immerse his will in deepest humility into God's mercy, and lay hold on such a will and resolution in the divine promise of grace, that he this very hour will depart from all ownhood of the pleasure of this world, and never enter any more therein; albeit he thereby should become the fool of all the world; he must wholly immerse himself into the deepest submissive lowliness and unworthiness before God with repentance, and yet in the soul apprehend and hold fast the promise of grace, and stand therein, as a soldier before his enemy, when it concerns his body and life.

8. When this comes to pass, then his own will (being the Antichrist) will be apprehended and mortified in the death of Christ, and his soul will soon become as a young simple child which has lost its natural understanding of selfhood, and begins to lament before God as a young

child before its mother, and trusts in the mother to give what she pleases to it.

9. And this is that, which Christ said, ye must turn and become as children, and forsake all and follow Me, for Adam departed from God's will into self-will, and has in his own self-desire brought the insinuations of the serpent and the will and desire of the devil into himself, so that he has brought himself and his life's comfort (which before stood in mutual harmony and agreement in one only will, which was God's) into a division and disunion, where the properties of nature departed from the equal agreement and concordance, each property entering into its selfhood (being an own or peculiar self-desire), whence the lust and imagination to good and evil did arise in him, and heat and cold presently fell on him, and he died from the holy life in the equal and mutual concordance, wherein he lived in one only pure element, wherein the four elements were in him in equal weight or temperature.

10. And of this God warned him, saying, *Eat not of the tree of the knowledge of good and evil, else you shall die*, meaning thereby the death to the kingdom of heaven, namely, the disappearance of the fair angelical image, which died presently in the false-introduced desire of the serpent; and therefore this false will of the serpent must first die in Christ's death by true conversion; and out of this death Christ arises in His spirit again in us in the heavenly image which died in Adam, and the inward man is regenerated and newborn in Christ's spirit

11. This new spirit comes to divine vision or contemplation in himself; it hears God's word and has divine understanding and inclination, and may behold the grand mystery, in divine and natural mysteries; and albeit

the earthly flesh yet cleaves to him in its inclination, yet does not at all hurt the newborn spirit in him.

12. He is in this new birth as solid fine gold in a rough drossy stone, the drossy soil of the stone being not able to destroy or spoil the gold: for his right will is dead to the earthly desire, and continually desires to kill and mortify the lust of the flesh, and does likewise kill it without intermission, for here the seed of the woman, viz., the new man born in Christ, bruises the head of the serpent's will in the flesh, which will is Antichrist.

13. And, beloved sir, I give you as a Christian and brother in all faithfulness, sincerity, and uprightness to understand that we in our supposed religion, wherein men do nothing but contend, confute, and revile one another about the scriptures and the different opinions thence contrived, are as yet in the midst of Babel and that it was never worse than now; and yet men boast that they have gone out from Babel and into the true religion.

14. But for so much as is known to me in the Lord my God, in my exceeding precious talent given to me of God, I say, that men indeed have dipped Christ's mantle with its purple color in the blood of Christ, and taken it upon them for a covering; and thereby they have only covered the antichristian child of self-will, and so have painted over the antichristian bastard with a strange color.

15. For men do exceedingly flatter it, and cover it with Christ's suffering merit, and death, and comfort it, that Christ has paid all for it, saying: It ought only to [apply or] comfort itself with the merit of Christ, and receive it in faith as a satisfaction, and thus they show us an outward imputed righteousness.

16. But it has far another A B C in the true understanding; no comforting, self-willing, running, or keeping a round, avails anything; the suffering, the death of Christ, will not be given to the antichristian beast in self, but to them that depart from, and relinquish all the ownhood [and propriety] of the creatures, and wholly resign up themselves into the suffering and death of Christ Jesus, and die to their own will, in and with Christ, and are buried with Him, and also arise in Him to a new will and obedience, and hate sin. Who put on Christ in His suffering, reproach, and persecution, and take His cross upon them, and follow Him under His Red Banner; to them I say, it will be given, these put on Christ in His process, and become in the inward spiritual man Christ's members, and the Temple of God, who dwells in us.

17. None has right to comfort himself with Christ's merits, unless he desires wholly to put on Christ in himself; and he is also no Christian before he has put Him on by true repentance and conversion to Him with an absolute resignation, and unfeigned self-denial; so that CHRIST espouses and betroths Himself with him.

18. The beginning of which comes to pass in the covenant of baptism, where the child promises and swears under Christ's Red Banner, that which afterwards must follow in very deed, or real practice; or if one has turned himself away [from the practice of what he then promised] he must in such a conversion of his will turn himself thereinto again; and I say upon sure ground that to many an one the mantle of Christ will turn to hellish fire, in that he covers Antichrist therewith, and yet remains but a beast.

19. For a Christian must be born of Christ, and die to the Adamic will; he must have Christ in him, and be a branch

or member on His flesh and spirit, not according to the animal beast, but according to the spiritual man.

20. For the spirit of God possesses not the beast [the outward sensual natural or rational man] but indeed the temple of Christ, viz., Christ's spiritual flesh and blood in us; for Christ said, *Whosoever shall not eat the flesh of the Son of Man, he has no life in himself.*

21. Now there must be a mouth which indeed is proper and fit to eat it, for it will not be given to the beast, much less to the *Ens* [moral essence] of the serpent; for every spirit eats of its mother, whence it is arisen; which I give to every understanding man to consider of, and here I only mention what a Christian ought to be, if he will account himself a Christian.

22. For a beast is no Christian, but he that is baptised with the Holy Ghost in the death of Christ; who has put on Christ, and lives in Christ's heavenly flesh and blood; who has tasted Christ's supper, and sits with Christ at table; he is a Christian that walks in Christ's footsteps, and continually mortifies the antichristian evil beast in flesh and blood (which still adheres to a Christian), binds it and deprives it of its strength, and patiently resigns himself up in temptations, which many hundred ways are offered him, for his trial and purification.

23. A Christian must learn the A B C backwards, and account the wisdom of his reason foolishness, that Christ may gain a form in him, and he be made capable of the heavenly wisdom.

24. For the wisdom of the outward world is blind in respect of God, and see Him not; albeit all things live and move in God, and He Himself is through all things, and yet He possesses nothing, save that which dies from its

own will, that He must possess, and He possessed it willingly; for it wills nothing without Him, and it is in the end of the creation, and also in the beginning.

25. Whereof I could further mention unto you, if occasion here did permit, the which I have in my writings largely described and declared out of the centre and original of all essences; and here only I have hinted in brief what a Christian's state, being, and condition is; if it should please you further to consider of it, and to give up yourself into this process, as I likewise hope that you are already in it.

26. But, for a more brotherly recreation, I thought good to visit you with a short epistle, and to solace myself a little with you in the hope and faith which works and is in us, until we be once freed from this cottage, and be afterwards refreshed and quickened perfectly, one with another, in divine and brotherly union and vision.

27. And this I have done upon the desire of the doctor abovementioned, in all sincerity and uprightness; and so I commend you to the tender love of Jesus Christ.

From THE WAY TO CHRIST, part three, The New Creation, chapter seven

158. A True Christian, who is born anew of the Spirit of Christ, is in the Simplicity of Christ, and has no Strife or Contention with any Man about Religion. He has Strife enough in himself, with his own Bestial evil Flesh and Blood. He regards himself a great Sinner, and is afraid of God: But the Love of Christ by degrees pierces through, and expels that fear, as the Day swallows up the Night.

159. But the Sins of the Impenitent Man rest in the Sleep of Death, bud forth in the Pit, and produce their Fruit in hell.

160. "Christendom," that is, Babel, strives about the Manner how Men ought to serve God, and glorify Him; also how they are to know Him, and what He is in His Essence and Will. And they preach positively, that whosoever is not one and the same with them in every Particular of Knowledge and Opinion, is no Christian, but a Heretic.

161. Now I would fain see how all their Sects can be brought to agree in that One which might be called a true Christian Church; when all of them are Scorners, every Party of them reviling the rest, and proclaiming them to be false.

162. But a Christian is of no Sect: He can dwell in the midst of Sects, and appear in their Services, without being attached or bound to any. He has but one Knowledge, and that is, Christ in him. He seeks but one Way, which is the Desire always to do and teach that which is right; and he puts all his knowing and willing into the Life of Christ.

163. He sighs and wishes continually that the Will of God might be done in him, and that His Kingdom might be manifested in him. He daily and hourly kills Sin in the Flesh; for the Seed of the Woman, viz., the inward Man in Christ, continually breaks the Head of the Serpent, that is, the Power of the Devil, which is in Vanity.

164. His Faith is a Desire after God and goodness; which he wraps up in a sure Hope, trusting to the Words of the Promise, and lives and dies therein; though as to the true Man, he never dies.

165. For Christ says, *Whosoever believes in me, shall never die, but has pierced through from Death to Life; and Rivers of living Water shall flow from him*, viz., good Doctrine and Works.

166. Therefore I say, that whatsoever fights and contends about the Letter, is all Babel. The Letters of the Word proceed from, and stand all in, one Root, which is the Spirit of God; as the various Flowers stand all in the Earth and grow by one another. They fight not with each other about their Difference of Colour, Scent, and Taste, but suffer the Earth, the Sun, the Rain, the Wind, the Heat and Cold, to do with them as they please; and yet every one of them grows in its own peculiar Essence and Property.

167. Even so it is with the Children of God; they have various Gifts and Degrees of Knowledge, yet all from one Spirit. They all rejoice at the great Wonders of God, and give Thanks to the most High in His Wisdom. Why then should they contend about Him in whom they live and have their Being, and of whose Substance they themselves are?

168. It is the greatest Folly that is in Babel, for People to strive about Religion, as the Devil hath made the World to do; so that they contend vehemently about Opinions of their own Forging, viz., about the Letter; when the Kingdom of God consists in no Opinion, but in Power and Love.

Compilation from THE LIFE AND DOCTRINE OF JACOB BOEHME by Franz Hartmann, chapter one
He alone is a true Christian whose soul and mind has entered again into the original matrix, out of which the life of man has taken its origin; that is to say, the eternal Word (Logos). This Word has been revealed in our human nature, which is blind to the presence of God, and he who absorbs this Word with his hungry soul, and thereby returns to the original spiritual state in which humanity took its origin, his soul will become a temple of divine love, wherein the Father receives His beloved Son.

In him will reside the Holy Ghost.

He alone, therefore, in whom Christ exists and lives is a Christian, a man in whom Christ has been raised out of the wasted flesh of Adam. He will be an heir of Christ—not on account of some merit gained by someone else, nor by some favor conferred upon him by some external power, but by inward grace.

To believe merely in a historical Christ, to be satisfied with the belief that at some time in the past Jesus has died to satisfy the anger of God, does not constitute a Christian. Such a speculative Christian every wicked devil may be, for everyone would like to obtain, without any efforts of his own, something good which he does not deserve. But that which is born from the flesh cannot enter the kingdom of the God. To enter that kingdom one must be reborn in the Spirit.

Not palaces of stone and costly houses of worship regenerate man; but the divine spiritual sun, existing in the divine heaven, acting through the divine power of the Word of God in the temple of Christ. A true Christian desires nothing else but that which the Christ within his soul desires.

All our religious systems are only the works of intellectual children. We ought to repudiate all our personal desires, disputes, science, and will, if we want to restore the harmony with the mother which gave us birth at the beginning; for at present our souls are the playgrounds of many hundreds of malicious animals, which we have put there in the place of God, and which we worship for gods. These animals must die before the Christ principle can begin to live therein. Man must return to his natural state (his original purity), before he can become divine.

There is no other way for Christ to live than through the death of old Adam; a man cannot become a god and remain an animal still. No one is saved by God as a mark of his gratitude for having attended church and having had the patience to listen to a sermon; but his attendance to external ceremonies can only benefit him if he hears Christ speak within his own heart.

All our disputations and intellectual speculations in regard to the divine mysteries are useless; because they originate from external sources. God's mysteries can be only known by God, and to know them we must first seek God in our own center. Our reason and will must return to the inner source from which they originated; then will we arrive at a true science of God and His attributes.

Man's will and imagination have become perverted from their original state, Man has surrounded himself by a world of will and imagination of his own. He has therefore lost sight of God, and can only regain his former state and become wise if he brings the activity of his soul and mind again in harmony with the divine Spirit.

A Christian is he who lives in Christ, and in whom Christ's power is active. He must feel the divine fire of love burn in his heart. This fire is the Spirit of Christ, who continually crushes the head of the serpent, meaning the desires of the flesh. The flesh is governed by the will of the world; but the spiritual fire in man is kindled by the Spirit. He who wants to become a Christian must not boast and say: *I am a Christian!* but he should desire to become one, and prepare all the conditions necessary that the Christ may live in him. Such a Christian will perhaps be hated and persecuted by the nominal Christians of his time; but he must bear his cross, and thereby he will become strong.

The theologians and Christian sectarians are continually disputing about the letter and form, while they care nothing for the spirit, without which the form is empty and the letter dead. Each one imagines that he has the truth in his keeping, and wants to be admired by the world as a keeper of the truth. Therefore they denounce and slander and back-bite each other, and thus they act against the first principle taught by Christ, and which is brotherly love. Thus the Church of Christ has become a bazaar where vanities are exhibited, and as the Israelites dance around the golden calf, so the modern Christians dance around their self-constructed fetishes, whom they call God, and on account of this fetish-worship they will not be able to enter the promised land.

All the teachings of Christ have no other object than to show us the way how we may reascend from a state of variety and differentiation to our original unity; and he who teaches otherwise teaches an error. All the doctrines which have been hung around this fundamental doctrine, and which do not conform with the latter, are merely the products of worldly foolishness, thinking itself wise; they are merely useless ornaments which will create errors, and are calculated to throw dust in the eyes of the ignorant.

Whoever presumes to set himself up as a spiritual teacher, and has no spiritual power of perceiving the truth, thinking to serve God by teaching the kingdom of God, of which he practically knows nothing, does not serve the true God, but serves his own self, and nurses and feeds his own vanity. He may have been legally appointed to his clerical office, and yet he is not a true shepherd. Christ says: *He who does not enter the stable of the sheep by the door, but enters by the window, is a thief and a murderer, and the sheep will not follow him, for they do not know his voice.* He is not in possession of the voice of God, but merely of the voice of his learning. But Christ said; *All plants which have not been planted by my heavenly Father shall be torn out and destroyed.* How, then, can he who is godless attempt to plant heavenly plants, having no spiritual seed and no power? To become a true spiritual teacher, one must teach in the Spirit of God and not in the spirit of selfishness.

A historical belief is merely an opinion based upon some adopted explanation of the letter of the written word, having been learned in schools, heard by the external ear, and which produces dogmatists, sophists, and opinionated servants of the letter. But Faith is the result of the direct perception of the truth, heard and understood by the inner sense, taught by the Holy Ghost, and productive of theosophists and servants of the divine Spirit.

IV. - FAITH

THE INCARNATION OF CHRIST: THE THIRD TREATISE

CHAPTER I

WHAT FAITH IS, AND HOW IT IS ONE SPIRIT WITH GOD

1. CHRIST says: *Seek ye first the kingdom of God and his righteousness, and all these things shall be added unto you* (Matt. vi. 33). Item: *My Father will give the Holy Spirit to them that ask him* (Luke xi. 13); *and when he is come, he will guide you into all truth; he will put you in*

mind of all that I have told you of; for he shall take of mine, and shall declare it unto you (John xvi. 13-15). Item: *I will give you a mouth and wisdom what ye should speak* (Luke xxi. 15). And St. Paul says: *We know not what we should pray and speak; but the Spirit of God intercedes powerfully for us, according to the pleasure of God* (Rom. viii. 26).

2. Now, faith is not an historical knowledge, that a man should frame articles to himself and depend on them alone, and force his mind into the works of his reason; but faith is one Spirit with God, for the Holy Spirit moves in the spirit of faith.

3. True faith is a power of God, one Spirit with God. It works in and with God. It is free and bound to no article, save only to true love, in which it gathers the power and strength of its life; human delusion and conjecture are of no consequence.

4. For as God is free from all inclination, in such a sense that he does whatever he wills, and needs to give no account about it: so also is the true right faith free in the Spirit of God. It has no more than one inclination, viz. to the love and mercy of God, so that it casts its will into God's will and goes out from the sidereal and elemental Reason; it seeks not itself in carnal Reason, but in God's love. And when in this way it finds itself, it finds itself in God, and works with God; not in acting according to Reason, whatever the latter will have, but in God, whatever God's Spirit will have. For it regards the earthly life as nothing, in order that it may live in God, and that God's Spirit in it may be the will and the doing. It gives itself up in humility to the will of God, and sinks down through reason into death, but springs up with God's Spirit in the life of God. It is as if it were a nothing, and yet in

God is all; it is an ornament and crown of the Deity, a wonder in the divine *magia*. It makes where there is nothing, and takes where nothing is made. It is operative, and no one sees its being; it uplifts itself, and yet needs no elevation. It is mighty, and yet is the lowliest humility. It possesses all, and yet embraces nothing more than gentleness. It is thus free from all iniquity and has no law, for the fierce wrath of nature has no influence upon it. It exists in eternity, for it is comprehended in no ground; it is impent in nothing, just as the unground of eternity is free and rests in nothing save in itself only, where there is an eternal tranquility.

5. So is it also with the right true faith in the unground. It is in itself essential being. It has life, and yet seeks not its life, but it seeks the life of the eternal calm tranquility. It goes out from the spirit of its life, and possesses itself: it is thus free from pain (*Qual*) as God is free from pain, and dwells thus in eternal freedom in God. It is with regard to the eternal freedom of God as a nothing, and yet is in everything. All that God and eternity is and is able to do serves it in some stead. It is laid hold of by nothing, and yet is a fair indwelling in the great might of God. It is a being, and yet is grasped by no being. It is a playmate and friend of the divine Virgin which is the wisdom of God; in it lie the great wonders of God. It is free from all things, just as light is free from fire, and though it is always generated by fire, yet the torment of fire cannot seize or reach it.

6. So in like manner we give you to understand that faith is begotten out of the spirit of life, as out of an ever-burning fire, and shines in that fire; it fills the fire of life and yet is never laid hold of. But if it be laid hold of, then itself has entered into reason as into a prison, and is no longer in God, in his freedom, but has entered into

torment; it torments itself, though assuredly it may become free. In reason it works wonders in the fire of nature, and in freedom it works the wonders of God in love.

CHAPTER II

OF THE ORIGIN OF FAITH, AND WHY FAITH AND DOUBT DWELL TOGETHER

1. SEEING then that faith is thus one Spirit with God, we are to consider its origin, for we cannot say that it is a figure or image of Reason. On the contrary, it is God's image, God's likeness, an eternal figure, and yet may be destroyed during the time of the body, or be transformed into source of anguish. For it is in its own nature, in the original state, merely a will, and the same will is a seed: this seed must the fire-spirit or soul sow in the freedom of God. In this way there grows from that seed a tree, of which the soul eats and appeases its fire-life, so that it becomes strong and gives its power to the root of the tree, whereby the tree grows up in the Spirit of God even unto the wonders of the Majesty of God, and buds in the Paradise of God.

2. And though by describing it we might be regarded as dumb and obscure, for Reason wants to see and to touch everything, we will reveal quite clearly why faith and doubt keep company and are as it were connected with a chain, so that there is a violent conflict in man all the time he is a guest in this tabernacle of the earthly life, unless he sink down so much in himself that he is able to introduce the fire of life into the freedom of God: then he is in the life of Reason as dead. Though he lives, he lives unto God, which indeed is a highly precious life of a man, and is seldom found in any, for it resembles the first image which God created. Although what is mortal still clings to

him, yet it is as it were dead, as if a dead image did cling to him which pertains to dissolution wherein the true man lives not. For the true life stands reversed, and is in another world, in another Principle, and lives in another source.

3. Understand us now in this way: You see and know the origin of human life, how it arises in the womb; and then you see in what it qualifies and moves, viz. in four forms; in fire, air, water and flesh. And though it lives thus therein, yet in such life it is no more than an animal life, for its reason comes to it from the stars, and it is found that the sun and stars make in the four elements a tincture, whence comes reason and qualifying-power, as well as pleasure and pain. But it is far from being the true human life, for natural reason seeks nothing higher than itself in its wonders. There is nevertheless in man a desire and a great yearning for a higher, better and eternal life, in which no such torment exists. And though reason grasps not nor sees this desire, yet in reason is a *mysterium* which tastes and knows that from which the craving springs. Thereby we recognize that this *mysterium* was implanted at the first creation and is man's own possession, as a desiring and yearning, a magical craving. Further, we find that with this *mysterium* we are in a strange lodging, and that the *mysterium* is not found in the spirit of this world, for the latter comprehends it not nor does it find it. By this we recognize the heavy fall of Adam. Then we find that this *mysterium* in the will of the soul is a hidden fountain which is revealed in another Principle. We understand moreover that this *mysterium* lies hidden in fire, in the source of anguish, and is disclosed through the anguish of the will. Thirdly, we find how the same *mysterium* is kept imprisoned by the spirit of this world and how the reason of the outer life has

power to enter into it and frustrate it, so that the *mysterium* does not attain to light but covers it up so that the genetrix [divine love] cannot bring forth, and so remains hidden in the *mysterium*. And when the body breaks, the will has not another which might reveal the *mysterium*; consequently the spirit of the soul, or fire spirit, remains in darkness, and the *mysterium* is eternally hidden in it as in another Principle.

4. We recognize, then, the *mysterium* as God's kingdom, which is hidden in the soul and gives to the soul a longing and desire, so that it imaginates into this *mysterium*, whereby it is impregnated magically in the same *mysterium*. Therefrom arises to it the will to go out from the fire-life into the *mysterium* of God. And if it uplift the will and cast it from it into the *mysterium*, the will is impregnated in the *mysterium*, for it has longing and acquires the body and essence of the *mysterium*, i.e. God's essence, which is incomprehensible to nature. Thus the will draws God's likeness or image to itself.

5. Seeing then that the will is begotten out of the soul's fire, it is indeed rooted in the soul, and there is no separation between the will and the soul. But the will becomes thus a spirit in God and becomes the soul's garment, so that the soul in the will is hidden in God, though it dwells in the body. It is thus in the will, which is the right earnest faith, a child of God, and dwells in another world.

6. This is not to be understood as an historical will, where Reason knows there is in it a desire for God, but keeps this desire imprisoned in wickedness, so that the will cannot go out from the soul and enter into the life or *mysterium* of God. This Reason forms opinions and involves the will in delusion, whereby the will cannot

attain the *mysterium* of God. It remains thus in delusion, or quite hidden in the soul, for it is directed towards something future, as Reason keeps the will a prisoner in the itch of the flesh, in the sidereal *magia*, and is always saying: Tomorrow thou shalt go forth and seek after the *mysterium* of God. In truth, there is no individual faculty of finding: this opinion deludes. In like manner freedom exists in no delusion where the will is able to enter and see God, in such a manner that Reason may imagine to itself to do something and so to be pleasing to God.

7. For there is no other way which can be more perfect than to go out with the will from Reason, and not will to seek oneself; but to cast oneself wholly into God's love and into God's will, and to let be all that Reason throws in the way. And though these were great sins and perpetrated vices, into which the body had entered, we should by the will only pass above them, and value God's love more highly than the filth of sin. For God is not a receiver of sins, but a receiver of obedience and of freewill. He suffers not sin within him, but a humble will which goes from the house of sin and wills no more sin, but sinks out of or beyond reason into His love, as an obedient humble child this child He receives, for it is pure. But if it still remains in delusion, it is encircled also with delusion, and is not free. Seeing then that God is in himself free from what is bad, the will also must be free, for thus it is God's likeness, image and own possession; for whatever cometh unto Him, into His freedom, He will not cast out, as Christ teaches us (John vi. 37).

CHAPTER III

OF THE PROPERTY OF FAITH, HOW IT GOES OUT FROM THE WILL OF THE NATURAL CRAVING INTO THE FREEWILL OF GOD

1. UNDERSTAND US further in this way: We know and recognize it in the Holy Scripture as well as by the light of nature that all comes from the eternal Being, viz. good and evil, love and wrath, life and death, joy and sorrow. We cannot on this account say that evil and death come from God, for in God is no evil nor any death, and to all eternity nothing that is bad enters into Him. Fierceness comes solely from the fire of nature, where life is found as in a *magia*, where each form of craving desires and awakens another. Therefrom arise the essences of plurality, from which wonders are generated wherein eternity manifests itself in similitudes. And yet we must say that in God's will is a desiring which gives rise to the *magia* wherefrom plurality springs. The plurality however is not God's will itself, which is free from all being; but in the craving of the will is brought forth nature with all the forms, so that all arises from the process of desire or from the eternal *magia*.

2. And we are further to know that all that which attains to life, which imaginates into the craving and places its will in nature, is the child of nature and one life with nature. But whatever with its will goes out from the craving of nature into the freewill of God is received and known of the Freewill, and is a spirit in God. And though it be in nature, just as nature has been generated from eternity in God's will, its spirit-life is nevertheless out of nature in the Freewill, and so the wonders of nature stand revealed in God, and yet are not God himself. And if the

spirit of the soul's will (the image) go out from the reason of nature into the freewill of God, then the spirit of the will is God's child and the nature-spirit God's wonder, and the creature is introverted on itself like God himself. Then the sidereal or reason-spirit seeks in its *magia*, in its centre of reason, the wonders of eternity, to which end God has created the soul in the body of the outer nature, though it is apprehended in the inner life alone. And the spirit of the will goes into the freedom of God, where then the Holy Spirit in the free divine *mysterium* leads it, so that the Deity is revealed in the spirit of the will, and in the reason-spirit is revealed the *magia* of nature with its wonders.

3. Seeing then the soul is the centre where the true spirit of the will, as distinguished from the freedom of God, proceeds into the freedom of God, as into the divine *mysterium*, it has also the sidereal spirit through connection. And if it tame this spirit, so that it work not wickedness, then it is able to introduce the sidereal wonders, which in the elemental mirror were made a substance, before the Majesty of God, into the freewill of God, so that the wonders appear in the freedom of divine Majesty as a likeness of the will of God. This is not to be understood as though the freedom of God commingles with the wonders of Nature and with the likeness so as to be One. No; God remains eternally free, he dwells in the wonders as the soul in the body. As little as the body lays hold of the soul, or the fire of the light, so little does Nature lay hold of the Deity. Yet it is a being and has from all eternity separated into two, even as fire and light, seeing that in fire we understand the source of nature, and in light the *mysterium* of the spirit-life without a source, albeit fire also is a *mysterium*.

4. Thus, understand us, it is also with regard to man. The

soul is the fire of the true human life which God breathed out in Adam with his spirit out of the eternal nature as out of the centre of God. And the spirit which was generated out of the soul fire, and was formed by God's spirit in his own image, this spirit has the divine *mysterium* from which the will to the love of God is generated, whence arises the divine *magia* or craving so that the will spirit craves for God. Now when it arises, that is, goes forth from the hidden *mysterium* into the freedom of God, it is a branch or growth in God's kingdom. It has grown out of God's *mysterium*, and works in God's will, and continually reveals the wonders in God's wisdom. Not in such a way as though in God something new were generated that was not from everlasting in God's wisdom, which has neither ground nor number, but alone in the spirit of the soul, in itself, does this eternal and infinite *mysterium* become revealed to God's honour and mirificence, and to its own, that is, the creature's, everlasting joy.

5. Since then the earthly and corrupt craving mingles with the sidereal source and the soul in the grievous fall of Adam has with its will imaginated into the stars as well as in the earthly craving and has introduced into itself the alien *magia*, therefore the will has been broken and the divine image destroyed. And the heavenly divine image of man became earthly, so that the right will is as it were turned about, that is in the spirit of this world, namely in the reason which is generated out of the stars. It is now needful for the true image of God which has thus been destroyed and has become earthly, that it should become other and be born again. And there would have been found no remedy for this image had not the Word out of the centre of God, that is God's own life, become man and had given a new birth in himself to the poor soul whose

image was now corrupted. Then was succour again given to the true image, else it would have been eternally robbed of the freedom and majesty of God.

6. And since all souls have proceeded from one, they have all been generated out of the corrupt root; but since new regenerated life in Christ has come into a soul again, it is needful for us all to cast our will into the regeneration through Christ. For in Christ we have been born again with our souls in God, and have attained again to the image. For after the Fall the *mysterium* in our soul stood only in the *magia* of nature which in its centre is a fire. And the image was turned out of the freedom of God into the outer *magia*, that is the external principle. Now when that breaks in pieces in the being the poor corrupt image of the soul stands bare, like a lost child; it can awaken in its own centre nothing but the fierce fire source. For it has gone out of the Word of God, that is God's *mysterium*, and has entered into a destructible mirror, that is the Spirit of this world, which has a beginning and an end. Wherefore also the soul's body has become wholly earthly and a prey to destructibility and death.

7. Now seeing that God has through grace turned his love to us and has in Christ turned the soul to himself into freedom, and has quickened the divine *mysterium* in the image so that the image can again dwell in God, that is in the wonders of paradise, it is needful for us to break off our will from the outer centre, that is from the transitory life, and to introduce it into the freewill of God. And for this is required not only a history or science, so that a man may say I believe that is, I know it or desire it, and nonetheless remains standing with his will in the external principle, that is in the outer craving. No, Scripture says, you must be born again through water and the Holy Spirit, else you will not see the kingdom of God (John 3:5).

There must be earnestness, the will of the reason must be broken, there must be a living movement of the will which breaks through reason and fights against reason. And though it is hardly possible for the soul, seeing it is very corrupt, yet there is no other and better remedy for it than to make itself as it were dead with all its reason and mind, and only to enter into and surrender itself to God's mercy that no room be left any more for reason, but that reason be mastered. And when the will thus beats down reason, reason appears as dead, though it still lives. But it becomes the servant of the right will, though out of it it would be master. For God's will must be master over reason if reason is to do any good that may subsist before God. For nothing subsists before God unless it be generated in God's will. But when the will turns towards God the will spirit becomes a child of God; then too the wonders which are done with the reason-spirit subsist before God, for they are done in God's will and are removed from that which has a beginning to the eternal.

8. And though we cannot well say that our works or achievements abide forever, yet there abides their shadow or image, although they remain truly in being. But that is in the *mysterium*, namely the divine *magia* before the wisdom of God against which only the outer principle breaks itself. For in the human image no more is broken than the outer dominion in the four elements, and the four are again set into one. Then also all colours and forms of the four elements are recognized with all which is generated therein. Therefore a final day of separation has been appointed by God in Nature when everything shall be tried by fire, whether it be generated in God's will or no, and when each principle shall reap its wonders. Then shall much of many a man's works remain in the fire because they were not generated in God's will, for in God

there enters nothing impure. But what has been generated out of another *magia* is not pure.

9. We have an example of this in the earth which is corrupt. If thou ask: Why? the answer is *The devil with his legions in his creation (though he was created an angel) sat in the Sulphur, or the centre of Nature, from which the earth was afterwards created.* It is the devil who has excited the wrath in Nature so that the earth has an evil, impure craving, although it is shut up in death and reserved for putrefaction. Then it will be tried in the everlasting fire, and come again into that state in which it was before the creation, namely into the eternal *magia* of the eternal nature.

CHAPTER IV

WHAT THE WORK OF FAITH IS AND HOW THE WILL MAY WALK THEREIN AND CONCERNING ITS GUIDE

1. SINCE then all that is generated out of nature is comprehended in God's will and we thus understand that nothing can enter God's will unless it be generated or made in God's will, we understand clearly that it is needful for us that we should with all our reason and mind give ourselves into God's will, and labour with our hands in the world and seek food for the belly, but not set our will therein at all, nor wish to account an earthly thing our treasure for where our will and heart are there also is our treasure. If our will is in God's will we have the great *mysterium* of God out of which this world was generated as a similitude of it. Thus we have both, the eternal and the perishable and yet more. We bring the wonders of our

works into the eternal *mysterium* for they cleave to the will-spirit. But when we turn aside our will from the eternal to the earthly *mysterium* and consider money our treasure, and the beauty of the body our glory, and honour or power as our fairest jewel, then our will is taken prisoner in it and thus we cling only to the mirror and do not attain to the freedom of God. For the mirror, which is the outer kingdom, shall be tried by fire and the wrath separated from the pure, for the wrath will be an everlasting burning.

2. Now when reason introduces the soul's mind together with the soul's will-spirit in which is the image of God and the true man into the external mirror, that is into a hypocritical craving, then indeed the image and the true man are made prisoner by it and infected with the outer *magia*, that is that same craving. For the image puts on the outer substantiality, not merely as a garment, but it is an infection and complete intermingling. For though the soul's fire does not mingle with the external kingdom, yet the soul's will-spirit which is of the *magia* is mingled with it and the image of God is destroyed and transformed into an earthly one, whereby the soul's fire life remains fierce and has an earthly image in the will-spirit.

3. Now when the body breaks up and dies the soul retains its image, that is its will-spirit. Now it is disjoined from the bodily image, for in death there is separation. Then the image appears together with and in those things which it has here taken into itself, with which it has been tainted, for it has the same source within itself. What it has loved here and what has been its treasure and what the will-spirit has entered into, according to this will the soul's image also be fashioned. If during his life a man has applied his heart and mind to pride, that same source will ever gush forth in the soul fire in the image and pass out

over the love and gentleness, that is God's freedom, and can neither lay hold of nor possess the freedom. But it gushes up in itself with such an anguishing torment and continuously fashions the will-spirit according to earthly things into which its will has entered. Thus it glitters therewith in the soul's fire and ever raises itself in pride and wishes to pass in the fire over God's gentleness, for it can create no other will. For it cannot enter into the freedom of God, into the holy *mysterium* wherein it might obtain another will, it lives only in itself alone. It has nothing, nor can it attain to anything but just that which it has in its outer life laid hold of in itself. So also it happens to the covetous man who has in his will and image the *magia* of the covetous craving. He always wants to have much and fashions to himself in the will-spirit that with which he has associated in the life of the body. But because the latter has forsaken him and his being is no longer earthly, he yet bears about with him the earthly will and plagues and torments himself with it, for he can attain to nothing else.

4. Far worse does it go with Falseness at which the wretched have cried out and have cursed the false man for his oppression. For whatever has been wrought in wickedness has been caused by him, it follows him, for it has been wrought in the *mysterium* of the wrath. Therefore the corrupt soul after the death of the body falls into it and must bathe in those same abominations. And if it were possible with the will to enter into the love of God, yet these same abominations and wickednesses hold it back, for they produce an everlasting despair, so that finally the soul becomes reckless, renounces God and desires only to rise up and to live in those abominations. And that is its joy: to blaspheme God and his saints, and but to exalt itself in the abominations above God and the

kingdom of heaven, and yet neither to lay hold of nor to see either.

5. Thus we give you to consider what are the will and confidence, viz. the master and guide, which introduce man's image both into God's love and God's wrath. For in the will is generated the right true faith in which stands the noble image of God; for in faith we are through Christ born again in God, and obtain again the noble image which Adam had lost and which Christ has again brought among mankind with the life of God.

6. A false will moreover destroys the image, for the will is the root of the image, it draws the *mysterium* of God into itself. And the spirit of that *mysterium* reveals that beautiful picture and clothes it with the divine *mysterium* which is God's substantiality, understand by this Christ's heavenly body which was born out of God in the dear and fair virgin of his wisdom, and which fills the heaven. If then our mind and will are set on that and the will desires it, then the will becomes magical and enters in. And if it hunger it may eat of the bread of God; now the new body grows upon it which is the blessed tree of the Christian faith, for every body loves itself. Now when the soul receives the body of God, which is so sweet and fair, how should it not love that which is given it for its own, in which it dwells and lives and of whose power it eats and by which it grows strong?

7. Thus no man should deceive himself and remain fixed in his falseness and unrighteousness, and take comfort in an historic faith by thinking: surely God is good, he will doubtless forgive me; I will gather treasure and enjoy it well and will leave to my children much wealth and honour, and later I will repent. But all this is pure deception. Thou gatherest for them falseness and drawest

into yourself unrighteousness. And though it still be done in the best way, yet it is earthly, for thou hast sunk your heart and will in an earthly vessel, thou hast clothed your noble image and infected it wholly therewith. Moreover thou leavest as an heritage to your children only pride, so that they also set their will-spirit on that alone. Thou thinkest to do good to yourself and your children and thou doest yourself and them the very worst.

8. It is true the outer life must have sustenance and he does foolishly who voluntarily gives his goods to the wicked. But far more foolishly does he who makes himself a wicked man with his goods, by setting his heart on them, and holding the temporal, transitory pleasure more in honour than the eternal abiding good which has no end. But that man brings blessing upon himself who comes to the help of the wretched, for they wish him all good and pray to God that He would bless him in body and soul. Thus their wish and blessing enter with the giver into the *mysterium* and surround him and follow him as a good work born in God. For this same treasure he takes with him, and not the earthly one. For when the body dies the image enters the *mysterium*, that is, it is revealed in the *mysterium* of God, for during the time of the earthly life the external principle has been a covering before it. Now this falls away with the dying of the body and then there appears the divine *mysterium* in the image and within it all the good deeds and works which have been generated by love in the will of God.

9. The wish and prayer of all good children of God are set in the *mysterium* and join themselves to the image, for the children of the wretched whom he has helped in their necessity and tribulations have sent their will in their prayer into God's *mysterium* and have therewith joined themselves to their deliverer and consoler and have given

him that straightway in the divine *mysterium*. So when that benefactor enters the *mysterium* and his earthly life falls away, then all things are revealed and each joins itself to its own to which the will has directed it.

10. All this will be reserved for the judgment of God the Holy Spirit in the *mysterium*, when each man shall reap what he has sown in his field here. Then it will all bud forth, grow and flower in a new heavenly earth, in which man will clothe his divine image with the body of the perfect *mysterium* of God; and before him, viz. before his bodily image, he will see standing his righteousness, and understand why he is so fair. He will know the cause of it and eternally rejoice thereat and frame his song of praise therein, to God's honour and mirificence. On the other hand the godless crowd will have scorn, envy, pride, malice and cursing of the wretched in their *mysterium* gathered together in the wrath, and these will follow them. Thus they will ever know the cause of their torment and therefore be eternal enemies of God and His children.

CHAPTER V

WHY THE UNGODLY ARE NOT CONVERTED; WHICH IS THE MOST PAINFUL PART OF CONVERSION; OF THE FALSE SHEPHERDS; HOW WE MUST ENTER INTO GOD'S KINGDOM; OF THE DESTRUCTION OF THE DEVIL'S KINGDOM; OF THE THREE FORMS AND WHAT WE HAVE INHERITED FROM ADAM AND CHRIST

1. THE ungodly crowd cannot now lay hold of all this, and the cause of it is that there is not the will in them which desires to lay hold on it, for the earthly being holds them bound so that they cannot obtain a will in God's *mysterium*. They are before God as the dead, there is no breath of the divine life in them. Nor do they desire it,

they are locked up in God's wrath *mysterium*, so that they do not know themselves. It is not God who has done this to them, but they have gone into it with their will-spirit and have sunk themselves into it thus; therefore they run like crazy men. Whereas the noble treasure is hidden within them in the centre, in the divine principle, and they might very well with their will pass out of the earthly being and wickedness into the will of God. They wilfully allow the wrath to hold them, for the proud and self-honouring life pleases them too well, and it is that which holds them.

2. But after this life there is no remedy for them anymore. When the soul-fire is bare and fierce it can be quenched by nothing but God's gentleness, that is, with the water of eternal life in the *mysterium* of God. But they do not attain to this for there is a great gulf between them, namely an entire principle. But in this life, while the soul as yet swims and burns in blood, it may well be, for the Spirit of God flies on the wings of the wind. God has become man, the Spirit of God enters the soul with the will, he desires the soul, he places his *magia* towards the soul; the soul need only open the door and he will enter voluntarily and open up the noble grain of the tree of Christian faith. But that is the most painful part, and the one which enters into man most hardly (if the tree of faith is to be generated in him), that he must lead the spirit of his will out of his earthly treasure, that is out of pride, covetousness, envy, wrath and falseness towards the Spirit of God. His mouth must not be a dissembler nor his heart and will remain fixed in the earthly *mysterium*: he must be in earnest from the ground of his heart and soul; the will must turn about into the divine *mysterium*, namely God's love, that the Spirit of God may have space and room in him to blow up the small divine spark. There

is no other remedy, and dissembling avails not.

3. Though a man should learn by heart all the Scripture, and sit all his life in church, but remain in his soul image an earthly and bestial man who is set only on falseness in his heart, his dissembling will avail him nothing. A preacher who acts outwardly according to God's *mysterium*, but has not God's image within, and is set only on honour and covetousness, is as close to the devil as the very meanest, for he is only a juggler with God's *mysterium*, and a dissembler without power. He himself has not God's *mysterium*, how then will he give it to others? He is a false shepherd, and a wolf among the sheep. For every man who bears God's *mysterium*, that is who has awakened it and has surrendered to it, so that God's Spirit drives him, he is God's priest, for he teaches from God. No man can teach aright unless he teach out of God's *mysterium*. But how will he teach who is outside it? Will he not teach from art and earthly reason? And what does that concern God's *mysterium*? Albeit reason is a noble thing, yet without God's Spirit it is blind. For Christ says: *Without me ye can do nothing* (John xv. 5). *Those whom God's spirit leads they are the children of God* (Rom. viii. 14). *He who climbs into the sheepfold by another way and not through Christ's spirit he is a thief and a murderer and comes only to rob and to steal* (John x. 1) and to seek his own profit. He is not a feeder of the sheep, but a devourer of them, like a wolf.

4. This is how we must understand concerning the tree of the Christian faith. It must be living and not a dead history or science. The word of life must be born a man in the image, so that the soul may bear God's image, else it is not God's child. It is of no use to be a hypocrite or to put off repentance upon hope, for so long as a man still bears the earthly image on his soul he is outside God's

mysterium. Nor may you think: I will indeed turn sometime, but I will previously gather enough for myself, so that I may not want and that earthly business may not afterwards lie in my way. No, that is the devil's trick. But it is through persecution, the cross, tribulation, scorn, contempt that we must enter into God's kingdom. For the devil holds sway in the earthly image and he mocks the children of God in his proud seat when they would escape from him. Therefore the wicked crowd serves the devil and helps him carry on his work.

5. The man who wishes to get to God must account all this as nothing. He must consider that he is in a strange country among murderers and that he is a pilgrim on the way to his true native land. He falls among murderers who torment and rob him, but so long as he carries off only so much that he preserve his noble image he has possessions enough, for in return for it he receives the heavenly *mysterium* within which lies everything and outside of which this world is but a mirror of it. Hence he is indeed most foolish who takes the reflection in a mirror for a substantial being, for the mirror breaks and its lover is bereft of it. He is like one who builds his house by a great water upon sand where the water carries away his house. So it is also with earthly hope.

6. O child of man, thou noble creature, do not yield it the power. It will cost thee thine eternal kingdom. Seek yourself and find yourself, but not in the earthly kingdom. How well does it truly befall him who finds himself in God's kingdom, who clothes himself in the heavenly and divine *mysterium* and enters into it! All the bravery of this world is filth in comparison with the heavenly, and is not worth that a man should fix his love upon it, although it be that it must be brought to a wonder to which end God has also created it.

7. Understand me: the outer man is to manifest the wonders of external nature, that is in the outer *mysterium*, both out of the earth and above the earth. All that the stars can do and the earth has in itself, all this man is to express in wonders, forms and being according to the eternal figure as has been seen in God's wisdom before the times of the world. But his will he is not to place therein, nor to consider it his treasure, but he may use it only for his ornament and delight. With his inner man he is to work in God's *mysterium*, then God's spirit will also help him seek and find that which is without.

8. Since then through the grievous fall we have been so corrupted that our mind has been turned from the heavenly *mysterium* into the earthly, that is the mirror, so that we are found to be as it were half dead, it is therefore most necessary for us that we go forth with our mind and will from the earthly glitter and seek ourselves first before we seek the earthly adornment, and that we first learn to know where we are at home and not make our mind earthly.

9. For man, though he be in God's image, is yet in a threefold life. But when he loses God's image, he is only in a twofold life, for the first life is that of the soul and arises in the fire of the eternal nature. And it stands chiefly in seven forms, all according to the spirit of nature. The second life stands in the image which proceeds from the fountain of the eternal nature, namely the soul's fire, the which image stands in the light in another source and has its living spirit as has been found with regard to fire and light. For the source of light is not the same as the source of fire and yet light proceeds from fire; and by the source of light we understand the gentle, pure and pleasant spirit, and by the source of the fire the causes of it. Thus it is seen that from the fire air arises

which is the spirit, and the air is also understood to be in four forms, viz. a dry one according to the fierceness of the fire, and a moist one as water from the astringent attraction. Thirdly, a gentle one from light and fourthly an upthrusting one from the fierce fire-terror. Thus we understand that light in all forms is master, for it has gentleness and it is a life which is generated through the bitter death, that is through the anguish source in the sinking down, that is another principle which exists in fire without feeling, and yet it has its feeling in itself, namely a pleasant taste. Thus we understand that water is generated through death, through the sinking down through the fire anguish. And we must further understand that it yet is no death, though it is *a* death. But the light causes it to bud forth so that there is life in it, which life stands in the power of light, seeing that life grows out of death, namely the substantiality, which is the comprehensibility, just as water which in itself is dead, but the fire life and the power of light is its life. Thus the substantiality is considered as dead, for the life within it is its own and possesses and generates itself within itself. And the death of the substantiality must give the body thereto. So we must by the light-life and the water of death understand two forms and according to the anguish in the fire the third. That is, first, in the anguish of the mortifying in the wrath of the fire we understand a fierce water, which with regard to the first four forms to nature, namely astringent, bitter, anguish and fire is like poison, and is indeed a poison, a hellish substantiality in the wrath according to the origin of the first principle, in which God's wrath springs up.

10. Secondly we understand the other water in the light-terror, in which the source sinks through the mortifying and in death becomes as it were a nothing, for in the

nothing the eternal freedom, that is the eternal abyss of eternity, is attained. Now when the ineffable light in that very sinking looks into eternity and always continues in the sinking down, the power of the light buds forth in the light and that is life coming forth from the sunk down death, for the wrath of the fire remains in the fiery source of the fierce water and does not go also into death. Nor can this be, for the fierceness is the strong almighty life that cannot die and cannot reach the eternal freedom, for it is called and remains forever the nature life. Although there is also a nature found in the light life, yet it is not painful or hostile as in the origin of nature in respect of which God calls himself a jealous wrathful God. For in the light source the water which through death has sunk into freedom becomes a source and water of the eternal life of joy, in which love and gentleness eternally flow upwards, and then it is no longer a sinking, but a budding forth which is called paradise. And the moving out from the source of the water is called Element, and that is the pure element in the angelic world. And the cause of the fire in light is the eternal firmament in which the eternal knowledge of God is manifested in wisdom, of which we have a similitude in the outer firmament and the stars.

11. Thus we understand two worlds one within the other, of which neither comprehends the other, namely one in the wrath of the fiery nature, in the water of poison and the anguish source wherein dwell the devils, and then one in the light in which the water of light has sunk down out of the anguish into the eternal freedom, and this the poison water cannot attain or lay hold of, and yet it is not separated except by death only, where it divides into two principles and falls into two lives: the one in the wrath and the other in the love, which life is known to be the true life in God. And in this lies the reason why, when

with Adam we went out from this (light) life into the outer (world) life, God became man. Thus he had through this death to bring us back through and out of the fierce source, out of the fiery anguish life, through death, into the light and love life. Though the gate of death was indeed locked in the wrath in the human soul, so that the soul was in the anguish source in the inner nature, in the fire of poison; that is the water of anguish, yet here did the Lord Christ break the lock of death, and with his human soul budded through death in the light of God and thus in his light-life now leads death captive, so that he has become a mockery. For with this lock Lucifer thought to be a master and almighty prince in the wrath; but when the lock was broken the power of the Deity in the light destroyed his kingdom. There he became a captive servant, for God's light and the water of gentleness are his death, for the wrath is killed thereby.

12. Thus have love and light entered the wrath with the paradisaical element and the water of eternal life, and thus God's wrath has been quenched. For this reason Lucifer now remains within himself as a mere anguished, wrath-filled fire source, in which his body is a poison and a source of the poison water. And thus he has been thrust out from God's fire into the matrix of the eternal nature, that is the harsh astringency which generates the eternal darkness. There he carries on the very stern government in the anguished Mercurius and is thus as one disgraced or cast out who in his origin was a prince. Now he is esteemed no more than an executioner or dishonourable villain who in God's wrath has to be as a hangman who punishes evil when he is bidden to do so by his lord. He has no further power, although he is still a deceiver and would like to lay hands on much so that his kingdom might become great, and that he might possess much and

not with little be a mockery. As also a whore thinks, *If only there are many whores then I shall not alone be a whore, but I am like others*; thus he too desires a great tribe that he may thereby mock God. The devil always lays the blame on God for his fall, saying that God's wrath had thus drawn him and thrust him into such a will of pride that he did not withstand. He thinks if only he might draw many to himself that his kingdom will grow great and that he will get all the more of them who also do as he does and would curse God, but justify themselves. That is his strength and delight in his dark and bitter anguish that he ever stirs up the fire within him and flies out above thrones. So he still regards himself as a lord and king; and though he is evil he is nevertheless a lord over his legions in the wrath in his creature. But with the wrath without his creature he has not power to act, there he must remain as an impotent captive.

13. Understand therefore the human life as being m two forms, one according to the fire of nature, the other according to the fire of light, the which fire burns in the love in which the noble image of God appears. And herein we understand that the will of man should enter into the will of God; thus he passes in the death of Christ and with the soul of Christ through death into the eternal freedom of God, into the light-life, and there he is with God in Christ. The third form of life is the outer life created out of the world, that is of the sun, the stars and elements, the which God's spirit breathed into Adam's nostrils with the spirit of the greater world, when he also became an outer soul, which swims in the blood and water and burns in the outer enkindled fire, namely in the warmth.

14. This outer life was not to enter into the image, viz. in the inner life, nor was the image to let it enter the inner

light (which shines through death and with its power buds in eternal freedom) for the outer life is only a similitude of the inner life. The inner spirit was only to manifest the eternal wonders in the outer mirror (such as in God's wisdom had been beheld in the unground in the divine *magia*) and to bring them into a figurative mirror, that is a wonder-mirror to God's honour and to the joy of the inner man who is generated of God. But his will was not to enter therein to draw the outer wonders into the image, as we now recognize with sorrow, that man draws into his mind and imagines an earthly treasure thus destroying the pure image of God according to the second principle.

15. For man's will-spirit now enters the earthly being and introduces his love in which the image resides into the earthly being, that is into an earthly treasure, an earthen vessel. Now the image in such an imagination also becomes earthly and passes again into death, and loses God and the Kingdom of Heaven, for its will-spirit remains fixed with its love in the outer life. Now the outer life must die and break up in order that the created image according to the inner kingdom may appear, and thus the will-spirit remains with its love in the outer wonders, and on the dying of the outer life brings these wonders with it before the judgment of God. There the will-spirit will have to pass through fire and the image be tried in the fire. All that is earthly must be burnt off from the image, for it must be quite pure and without spot. Just as the light subsists in the fire, so the will-spirit must also subsist in God's fire, and if it cannot pass unhindered through the fire of God, through death, that same soul image will be spewed out into eternal darkness.

16. And just this is the grievous fall of Adam that he placed his will-spirit in the outer life, that is the external principle, in the false craving, and imaginated into the

earthly life. Thus he went out from paradise which, through death, buds forth into the second principle, into the Outer, and thus he entered into death. He had therefore to die, and thus his image was destroyed. This we have inherited from Adam. But we have also inherited the regeneration from the second Adam, Christ, in that we must enter into the incarnation of Christ and go with him into his death and with him out of death bud forth in the paradise world in the eternal substantiality of the freedom of God.

CHAPTER VI

WHAT LUST CAN DO; HOW WE IN ADAM HAVE FALLEN AND IN CHRIST HAVE BEEN BORN AGAIN; AND THAT IT IS NOT SUCH AN EASY MATTER TO BECOME A TRUE CHRISTIAN

1. THUS we understand that it is due to lust, and that corruption has come out of lust and still does so. For lust is an imagining in which the imagination insinuates itself into all forms of nature so that they are impregnated with the thing out of which lust springs. By this we understand the outer spirit of man which is a similitude of the inner. It has lusted after the fair image and for its sake has set its imagination on the inner, whence the inner has become tainted. And because it did not immediately feel death it has made room in its will-spirit for the outer. Thus the outer has taken up its lodging in the inner and has finally become the master in the house, and has darkened the inner so that the fair image has faded. Here the fair image fell among murderers, that is, among the harsh spirits of nature and the origin of life. These held the image captive and drew off from it the robe of paradise and left it lying half dead.

2. Now was there need of the Samaritan, Christ. And that is the cause that God became man. If the harm could have been healed through the speaking of a word or a word of forgiveness God would not have become man. But God and paradise were lost and moreover the noble image had been destroyed and made desolate and had to be generated again out of God. Therefore God came with his word which is the centre in the light-life, and became flesh, so that the soul might again receive a divine paradise-dwelling. Understand that as Adam's soul had opened the door of the fire-essences and let in the earthly essences (the which source had insinuated itself into the paradise-image and made the image earthly), so God's heart opened the door of the light-essences and clothed the soul with heavenly flesh, and thus the essences of the holy flesh imaginated after the image, after the soul's essences. Thus the soul was once more impregnated so that with its will-spirit it entered through death into the paradise-life. Hence came the temptation of Christ, that he was tempted to see whether the soul would eat of the Word of the Lord, and could, through death, enter again into God's life. And this was finally fulfilled on the tree of the cross when Christ's soul passed through the fire of wrath, through the stern source, through death and budded forth again in the holy paradise world in which Adam was created. Thus were we men helped again.

3. Therefore it is needful for us that we should draw out our will, mind and heart from all earthly things and turn them into Christ's suffering, dying, death and resurrection, that we continually crucify the old Adam with Christ's death and continually die with sin in the death and dying of Christ and with him continually rise again out of the anguish of death into a new man and bud forth in the life of God. There is no other remedy but this. We must die to

the earthly world in our will, and must continually be born again in faith to the new world in the flesh and blood of Christ. We must be born out of Christ's Flesh if indeed we will see the kingdom of God.

4. It is not such an easy matter, but the hardest thing of all, to be a true Christian. The will must become a champion and must fight against the corrupt will. It must sink itself out of the earthly reason into the death of Christ, in God's wrath, and, as a worthy champion, break the power of the earthly will and venture so desperately that it will stake its earthly life on it and not desist until he has broken the earthly will. And that is indeed a stern warfare in which two principles struggle for the mastery. It is no jest: there must be determination to fight for the knightly garland, and no man attains to it unless he be victorious. He must break the power of the earthly will which, however, he is unable to do of his own might. But, if he sink himself out of the earthly reason with his inner will into Christ's death, he will sink through Christ's death, through God's wrath, into the paradise world, into the life of Christ in spite of all opposition of the devil. He must make his will as it were dead; thus he will live to God and sink into God's love, while yet he lives in the outer kingdom.

5. But I speak of the knightly garland which he will receive in the paradise world when once he penetrates into it. For there the noble seed is sown and he receives the most precious pledge of the Holy Spirit which afterwards leads and guides him. And though in this world he have to walk in a dark valley where the devil and the wickedness of the world always roar over him and often cast the outer man into abominations and thus cover up the noble grain of mustard seed, yet it will not let itself be kept back, but buds forth, and there grows from it a

tree in God's kingdom despite all the raging and roaring of the devil and his followers. And the more the noble pearl-tree is crushed down, the more vigorously and mightily it grows. It will not let itself be suppressed even though it should cost the outer life.

6. Therefore, my dear soul, inquire aright after the tree of Christian faith. It does not stand in this world. It must indeed be within thee, but thou with the tree must be with Christ in God, in such a way that this world merely hangs on thee as it also only hung on Christ. But this must not be understood to mean that this world is worth nothing or is unprofitable before God. It is the great *mysterium*, and man has been created into this world, as a wise ruler of it, that he should disclose all its wonders (which from everlasting are in the sulphur out of which this world with the stars and elements have been created) and to bring them according to his will into forms, figures and images, all to his joy and glory.

7. Man was created entirely free without any law. He had no law but the nature-law alone, that he should not mingle one principle with the other. The inner man was to allow nothing earthly to enter into him, but was to rule all-powerfully over the outer principle. Thus there would have entered into him neither death nor dying, nor could the outer elements have touched him, neither heat nor frost would have touched him. For as the noble image must subsist in the fire, so also that noble image was to rule throughout the whole man, through all three principles, and govern all and fill all with the source of paradise.

8. But as that might not be and the flesh has become earthly, we must now be generated in the faith, seeing that indeed the earthly life covers the true life. We must

therefore put on the right garment called Hope and set our will on hope and always labour at the tree of faith that it may bring forth its fruits, namely the blessed love towards God and our neighbour. A man must be good, not only for his own sake, but also that he may through his example and life amend his neighbour. He must consider that he is a tree in God's kingdom, so that he may bear God's fruit, grow in God's field, that his fruit is for God's table, and that he may clothe his works and wonders in true love and walk in love that he may bring them into God's kingdom. For God is a spirit and faith is also a spirit in God and God has become man in Christ. The faith's spirit is also in Christ born a man. Thus the will-spirit walks truly in God, for it is one spirit with God, and with God works divine works. And though the earthly life cover him so that he does not know the works which he has generated in faith, yet, in the destruction of the earthly life, it is made manifest, for hope is his shrine and a mystery in which the works of faith are sown and also preserved.

CHAPTER VII

TO WHAT END THIS WORLD WITH ALL BEING WAS CREATED, ALSO CONCERNING TWO ETERNAL MYSTERIES; OF THE EXCEEDINGLY FIERCE STRUGGLE IN MAN FOR THE IMAGE, AND WHEREIN THE TREE OF THE CHRISTIAN FAITH STANDS, GROWS AND BEARS FRUIT

1. SINCE man thus stands in a threefold life, each life is a *mysterium* to the other and each desires the other. For this end the world with all Being has been created, for the divine essentiality desires the mirror or similitude. For this world is a similitude according to God's being, and God is revealed in an earthly similitude. For the wonders

of the hidden secrecy might not be disclosed in the angelic world, in the love-birth. But in this world in which love and wrath are mingled, where there is a twofold genetrix, it might be. For all things originated out of the fire root but are surrounded with the water of gentleness, so that it is a lovely being. But since in the angelic world the fire is not known, for the centrum of the genetrix stands in the light and is God's word, the wonders of nature cannot be manifested otherwise than in a spiritual *magia*, that is, they must be seen in God's wisdom. But as this is almost impossible for the angels and the souls of men to lay hold of, and yet God wills to be known of angels and men, the angelic world yearns for the great wonders to know them which from eternity have been in God's wisdom. And in the earthly similitude these are brought into substance, in figures and images, all of them according to the eternal essences of the centre of nature, so that the wonders may abide forever. Not however essentially, but in figures, images and similitudes, and in forms. Magical indeed according to the will, but the genetrix is nonetheless in the centre of the wonders, for it has once been awakened out of the fire, but it will be swallowed up again in the *mysterium* and stands as a hidden life. Therefore all beings shall be made manifest as a shadow in the angelic world, but only those which in God's will have been introduced into the *mysterium*. For there are two mysteries which are eternal, the one in love, the other in wrath. Into whichever of these the will-spirit with its wonders enters, there within also stand all its works and wonders.

2. In the same manner therefore we are to know that the outer vehemently desires the inner, for all runs toward the centre, that is, the origin, and desires freedom. For in the fire of nature there is anguish and torment; now therefore

the formation or image of the gentleness in the source of love wills to be free, and yet may not be free in the source of the fiery essences, until the time when the source divides in the breaking: then each passes into its *mysterium*. In like manner the fire wants to be free from the water, for water is also the fire's death, and is also a *mysterium* for it. Similarly we see herewith how the water holds captive the fire, and yet there is no dying in the fire, but it is only a *mysterium* in the fire, as can be see when it breaks out in the water and manifests itself, when it reveals itself out of the centre of its own genetrix. This may be seen in the lightning, and may also be recognized in a stone, which yet is water. We see however chiefly how all forms of nature desire light, for in that desire is generated the oil in which the light becomes known, for it originates from the gentleness.

3. Our life is thus to be known to us, namely, that in us the centre of fire stands open, for the life burns in the fire. And then we have to consider the desire for love which originates in the word of life in the angelic world where God's heart with its desiring stands towards us with its imagining and also draws us into the divine *mysterium*.

4. And thirdly we must consider the magical kingdom of this world which also burns in us and draws us vehemently into its wonders, for it wills to be manifest. And man was created therein to this end that he should reveal that same *mysterium* and should bring the wonders to light and into forms according to the eternal wisdom. Now seeing he is to do this and thus burns in a threefold fire, the true spirit, in which the angelic image dwells, has great anxiety and is in great danger, for it walks along a very narrow path and has two enemies which continually draw it, each of which wants to be in the image and to introduce its source therein. These are the inner and the

outer fire; the inner kingdom of wrath and also the outer earthly kingdom of the mirror. Thus the true image stands in the midst in the crush. For the inner kingdom wants to manifest the wonders through the outer one, but because it is too sharp the outer kingdom flees from the inner and grasps at the middle, namely the image, which stands in the freedom of God, and so entwines itself into the image. For it all reaches out to the heart of God as to the centre of the kingdom of joy. Now the image has need to defend itself that it let not in the earthly guest, much less the fiery one. And yet it is generated out of both, that is, the life out of the fire and the wonders out of the outer life. Therefore it is most necessary for man's image that it lead a temperate sober life and not fill itself too full of the outer kingdom, else this will make its indwelling in the noble image.

5. And here we understand the mighty struggle in man for God's image, for there are three that strive for it. First the stern fire-life, secondly the divine life, and thirdly the earthly life. Thus the noble image stands in the middle and is drawn by three. Now it is needful for it to hide itself in faith in the *mysterium* of hope and stand still in that *mysterium* seeing that the devil in the inner fire-life continually rides forth into the outer earthly life in pride, falseness and covetousness, over the noble image, and would bring it into the fire and anguish life and break it. For he always thinks that the place of this world is his kingdom; he will suffer no other image therein. Now the noble image falls into suffering, tribulation, anguish and distress, and at this point a great struggle ensues to fight for the noble knightly garland of God's image. Hence arises prayer that the image may ever go forth with prayer out of the introduced earthly being, and also out of the proud, hellish abominations, continually enter into God's

life, and his love. Thus the true image continually slays the earthly Adam as well as the hellish devil of pride, and must continually stand as a champion. The most necessary thing for it is to wrap itself in patience, to throw itself under the cross and ever to well up in love, for that is its sword with which it slays the devil and drives out the earthly nature. It has no other sword with which to defend itself than the sweet water of the eternal life; which the proud fierce fire-spirit does not relish, for it is poison to it and it flees from it.

6. Now if we wish rightly to make known the tree of the Christian faith we say: Its root stands in the *mysterium* of hope, its growth in the love and its body in the laying hold of faith, that is when the image with its earnest desiring penetrates into God's love and grasps the substantiality of God, namely Christ's body. This is then the corpus in which the tree stands, grows and buds and brings forth fruits in patience. All of these fruits belong to the angelic world, they are the food of the soul, of which the soul eats and refreshes its fiery life so that it is changed into the light of gentleness.

7. Thus grows the tree in God's paradise, a tree which the outer man does not know, and which no reason grasps, but to the noble image it is very well known. When the outer life is broken up. the tree is then manifest and all its works follow it in the *mysterium* of hope into which it has sown. Therefore let no one who will follow God's pilgrim's way purpose to have in this world good and gladsome days with worldly honour, but tribulation, scorn and persecution await him every hour. Here he is only in a vale of misery and must continuously stand in strife, for the devil goes about him like a roaring lion and incites all his children of wickedness against him. He is accounted a fool, he is a stranger to his brother, his mother's house

scorns and despises him. He passes along, sows in tribulation, suffers anguish, but there is no one who understands or whose heart is moved thereby. Everyone deems it is his folly which thus plagues him. Thus he remains hidden to the world, for with his noble image he is born, not of the world, but of God. He sows in sorrow and reaps in joy. But who can express the glory which is his reward? Or who will speak of the knightly garland which he attains? Who can express the virgin's crown which the virgin of God's wisdom sets upon him? Where is there such beauty which surpasses Heaven? Oh noble image! Thou art indeed an image of the Holy Trinity in which God himself dwells. God sets upon thee his fairest jewels that thou mayest eternally rejoice in him.

8. For what then is the nature of this world seeing that it breaks up and only brings man into grief, anguish and misery, moreover into God's wrath, destroys his fair image and clothes him in a monstrous shape? Oh, what great shame will a man have on this account, when at God's judgment-day he will appear thus with a bestial image, not to speak of what follows thereafter, that he shall remain therein eternally. Now will begin a repentance, a groaning and weeping for the lost pledge which cannot in all eternity be recovered, for the image has to stand eternally before the horrible devil and do what Lucifer, the prince of abominations, will.

CHAPTER VIII

IN WHAT MANNER GOD FORGIVES SIN, AND HOW YOU BECOME A CHILD OF GOD

1. MY dear, seeking, eager mind, that hungers and thirsts for God's kingdom, do give heed to the ground of what is shown you. It is indeed not so easy a matter to become a child of God as Babel would have you believe. There,

consciences are led into histories, they are flattered with Christ's sufferings and death; there the forgiveness of sins is taught historically as in a worldly court of law, there guilt is remitted through favour, though a man remain a hypocrite at heart. Here it is altogether different; God will have no hypocrites. He does not thus take our sins from us while we cling only to *science* and comfort ourselves with the sufferings of Christ, but in our *conscience* remain in the abominations. Scripture says: *Ye must be born again or ye will not see the kingdom of God.* A man who should flatter himself with Christ's sufferings and death, and appropriate that to himself, but with his will should remain unregenerate in the Adamic man, is like one who comforts himself that his master will bestow his land on him though he be not his son, and though the master have promised to bestow it on the son alone. Thus it is here also. Wilt thou possess your master's land and have it for thine own thou must become his true son, for the son of the maidservant shall not inherit with the son of the free woman. The son of History is a stranger; thou must be born of God in Christ that you may become a true son; then thou wilt be God's child and an heir to the suffering and death of Christ. Christ's death is your death, his resurrection from the grave is your resurrection, his ascension your ascension, and his eternal kingdom your kingdom. In that thou art born his true son of his Flesh and Blood thou art an heir to all his goods. Thou canst not otherwise be the child and heir of Christ.

2. So long as the earthly kingdom remains in thine image thou art the earthly son of the corrupt Adam. No dissembling avails. Give fair words before God as thou wilt, thou art none the less an alien child and God's goods are not your due until thou return with the prodigal son to the father in right true contrition and repentance for your

lost heritage. Then thou must with your will-spirit go out from this earthly life and break the earthly will; (it hurts to forsake with the mind and will-spirit the treasure once possessed, in which the will-spirit was generated), and thou must enter into God's will-spirit. There thou wilt sow your seed in God's kingdom and wilt be born again in God as a fruit which grows in God's field, for your will receives God's power, Christ's body and the new body in God will grow on thee. Then art thou God's child and Christ's goods belong to thee. His merit is your merit, his suffering, death and resurrection, all are thine, thou art a member of his body, his Spirit is your spirit, he will lead thee in the right way and all thou doest, thou doest to God. Thou sowest in this world and reapest in God's heaven; thou art God's wonder-work and thou revealest his wonders in the earthly life and drawest them with thy will-spirit into the holy *mysterium*.

3. Mark this therefore, ye covetous, proud, envious, false judges, ye wicked men, who bring your will and desire into earthly goods, money and possessions, into the sweets of this life and account money and possessions your treasure and set your desire therein, though ye want nonetheless to be God's children; ye stand and dissemble before God that he may forgive you your sins. But with your image ye remain in Adam's skin, in Adam's flesh, ye comfort yourselves thus with Christ's suffering and are but dissemblers. Ye are not God's children, ye must be born in God if ye will be children, else ye deceive yourselves together with your hypocrites who paint deceptive colours before you. They teach, but are not known of God, nor sent to teach. They do so for the belly's sake and for worldly honour, and they are the great whore in Babel who dissemble to God with their lips, but with their heart and will-spirit serve the dragon in Babel.

4. Dear soul, if you would become God's child, prepare for temptation and tribulation. It is not easy and pleasant to enter into the child-life, especially when reason lies imprisoned in the earthly kingdom. The reason must be broken, and the will go forth from the reason and sow itself in humble obedience in God's kingdom, as a grain is sown in the field. The will must make itself as it were dead in reason and give itself up to God; thus the new fruit grows in God's kingdom.

5. Man therefore stands in a threefold life and all belongs to God; the inner fiery essences of the first principle are incorporated with the new body in Christ, so that they may out of God's will flow into Christ's flesh and blood. Their fire is God's fire out of which burn love, gentleness and meekness, whence goes forth the Holy Spirit and helps them sustain the battle against earthly reason as also against the corrupt flesh and the devil's will. Man's yoke of the earthly will becomes easier to him, but he must in this world remain in the strife. For to the earthly life belongs sustenance; this man must seek and yet he may not set his will and heart upon it and cleave to it; he must trust in God, his earthly reason continually falls into doubt that he may suffer lack; it desires continually to see God and yet cannot, for God dwells not in the earthly kingdom but in himself.

6. Therefore reason, because it cannot see God, must be driven into hope; and there doubt runs counter against faith and would destroy hope. Then the earnest will must fight with the true image against the earthly reason. That is painful and it often goes sadly, especially when reason considers the course of this world, and recognizes its will-spirit as foolish in respect of the course of this world. Then scripture says: *Be sober, watch, fast and pray that ye may benumb the earthly reason, and make it as it were*

dead that God's spirit may find place in you. When it appears it soon overcomes the earthly reason and looks with its love and sweetness at the will in its anguish, and each time a fair little branch is then generated out of the tree of faith, and all tribulation and temptation serve God's children for the best. For whenever God ordains for his children that they be brought into anguish and tribulation they stand each time in the birth of a new branch out of the tree of faith. When the Spirit of God appears again it draws up each time a new growth whereat the noble image greatly rejoices. It is only a question of the first serious onslaught when the earthly tree must be overcome and the noble grain sown in God's field, so that man may learn to know the earthly man. For when the will receives God's light the mirror sees itself in itself, one essence sees the other in the light. Thus the whole man finds himself in himself and knows what he is, which he cannot know in the earthly reason.

7. Therefore let no one think that the tree of Christian faith may be seen or known in the kingdom of this world. The outer reason knows it not, and although the fair tree stands already in the inner man, yet the outer, earthly reason still doubts, for the Spirit of God is to it as foolishness, which it cannot grasp. Although it may happen that the Holy Spirit reveal himself in the outer mirror so that the outer life greatly rejoices therein and becomes trembling for great joy and thinks: Now I have won the worthy guest, now I will believe it, yet there is no perfect continuance therein, for the Spirit of God does not remain evermore in the earthly source. He will have a pure vessel, and when he withdraws into his principle, namely the true image, the outer life becomes despondent and timorous. Therefore the noble image must always be in strife against the outer reason-life, and the more it

strives, the greater grows that fair tree, for the image cooperates with God. For just as an earthly tree grows in wind, rain, cold and heat, so also the tree of God's image amid suffering and tribulation, in anguish and pain, in scorn and contempt, and buds forth in God's kingdom and brings forth fruit in patience.

8. Seeing then we know this we should apply ourselves thereto and not let ourselves be held back by any fear or terror, for we shall indeed enjoy and reap to all eternity what we have sown here in anguish and hardship, so that we have comfort eternally. Amen, Hallelujah!

THE INCARNATION OF CHRIST CHAPTER XIII

1. ALL that is taught, written, preached or spoken in the old Adam regarding Christ, whether it be as the result of art or no matter how, belongs to death, and has neither understanding nor life; for the old Adam is dead as to Christ. The new Adam only, who is born of the virgin, should do this; he alone understands the word of regeneration and enters by the door of Christ into the sheepfold. The old Adam aims at getting in by art and inquiry. He supposes that Christ may be grasped sufficiently in the letter. He holds that one who has learned arts and languages, who has read much, is appointed by God and called to teach; that the Spirit of God must speak through his preaching, even though he is but the old corrupt Adam. But Christ says: *These are robbers and murderers, and have come only to rob and to steal. He that entereth not by the door into the sheepfold, but climbeth up some other way, the same is a thief and a murderer* (John 10:1). And he says *further I am the door of the sheep: by me if any man enter in, he shall find*

pasture, and the sheep will follow him (John 10:9). *For he that is not with me is against me.*

2. A teacher must necessarily be born of Christ, otherwise he is a thief and a murderer, and only stands forth to preach for the belly's sake. He does it for money and honour, he teaches his own word and not God's word. But if he is born again of Christ, he teaches Christ's word, for he lives in the tree of Christ, and gives his sound from the tree of Christ, in which he lives. Therefore is there such contrariety on the earth, because men heap to themselves teachers, to tell them what their ears itch after and what the old evil Adam readily listens to, what ministers to his elevation and carnal pleasure, what is conducive to might and magnificence.

3. O ye devilish teachers, how will you stand before the wrath of God? Why do you teach, when you are not sent from God? You are sent from Babel, from the great whore, from the mother of the great spiritual whoredom on earth. Not of the virgin are ye born, but of the adulterous woman. For not only do ye teach human fictions, but also persecute the teachers that are sent, who are born of Christ. You contend about religion, and yet there is no contention in religion: there are diversity of gifts, but one and the same spirit speaks. As a tree has manifold branches and the fruit has a manifold form, not being just like one another; or as the earth bears diverse herbs and flowers, the earth being the one mother so is it with those who speak by God's spirit; each of them speaks from the wonder of his gifts. But their tree or their field, upon which they rest, is Christ in God. And you, binders of the spirit, will not suffer this. You insist on stopping the mouth of your Christ, whom yet you yourselves teach unknown with the earthly tongue, and insist on binding him to your law. Oh, the true church of Christ has no law!

Christ is the temple where we must enter. The heap of stones does not make a new man. But the temple of Christ, where God's spirit teaches, awakens the half-dead image, so that the image begins to bud. It is a matter of indifference, God cares not for art or for eloquence, but *he that cometh to Him He will in no wise cast out*. Christ came into the world to call and save poor sinners; and Isaiah saith: *Who is so simple as my servant?* Therefore the wisdom of this world will not do, it only brings about pride and puffed up reason, it has high pretensions and wishes to lord it. But Christ says: *He who forsakes not houses, lands, goods, money, wife and child, for my name's sake, is not worthy of me*. All that is in this world should not be so dear as the precious name Jesus. For whatever this world has is earthly, but the name Jesus is heavenly, and out of the name Jesus we must be born again from the virgin.

4. Therefore the virgin's child is opposed to the old Adam. The latter shows himself by desires of temporal pleasure, honour, power and authority, and is a fierce, horrible dragon, who seeks only to devour, as the Revelation of John represents him. The child of the virgin, however, stands upon the moon, and wears a crown of twelve stars; for it treads under foot what is terrestrial or the moon; it has grown forth from the terrestrial moon like a flower from the earth. Accordingly the virgin image stands upon the moon. Against it the fierce dragon casts out of his mouth water as a flood, and tries continually to drown the virgin image. But the earth comes to the aid of the virgin and swallows up the flood of water and brings the virgin into Egypt, where the virgin image must suffer itself to be put into servitude. But the earth, or the wrath of God, covers the virgin image and swallows up the torrent of the dragon. And though the dragon overwhelms with his

abominations the virgin image, calumniates and reviles it, yet this does not do the child of the virgin any harm; for the wrath of God receives the reviling which is poured out upon the pure child, the earth always signifying the wrath of God. Thus the virgin child stands on the earth, that is, on the terrestrial moon, and must always flee from the earthly dragon into Egypt. There it must be in bondage to Pharaoh; but it stands upon the moon, not under. The prince Joshua or Jesus brings it through Jordan to Jerusalem. It must by death enter into Jerusalem and quit the moon. It is but a guest in this world, a stranger and pilgrim; it has to journey through the dragon's country. When the dragon shoots forth his torrent upon it, it must bow down and put itself under the cross; then the wrath of God receives the dragon's fire.

5. It is known to us that the old Adam knows and understands nothing of the new; he understands everything in an earthly way. He knows not where or what God is; he. acts the hypocrite to himself, ascribes to himself piety and thinks that he serves God, yet serves only the old dragon; he sacrifices, and his heart cleaves to the dragon; he will be genuinely devout and with what is earthly ascend into heaven, and yet mocks at the children of heaven. Thereby he shows that he is an alien in heaven; he is only a master on earth and a devil in hell.

6. Among such thorns and thistles must the children of God grow. They are not known in this world, for the wrath of God covers them. Even a child of God knows not himself aright; he sees only the old Adam who hangs unto him, who always strives to drown the child of the virgin. Unless indeed the virgin's child obtain a glimpse into the *Ternarius Sanctus*; then he knows himself, when the fair knightly garland is set upon him; in such case must the old Adam look on from behind, and knows not what

happens to him. He is indeed joyful, but he dances as one who dances to the sound of stringed instruments: when the playing ceases, his joy has an end and he continues to be the old Adam; for he belongs to the earth and not to the angelic world.

7. As soon as a man gets to the point that the virgin image begins to bud forth from the old Adam, so that the man's soul and spirit gives itself up into the obedience of God, then in him does the combat begin, for the old Adam in the wrath of God fights against the new Adam in the love. The old Adam wishes to be lord in flesh and blood, and in this connection the devil can reach, infect and possess him. The virgin twig can the devil not endure, but he may not touch it. Because his own dwelling in the darkness of the abyss pleases him not, he willingly dwells in man; for he is an enemy of God and outside of man has no power. Therefore he possesses man, and leads man as he pleases into the anger and wrath of God, so that he may mock at God's love and gentleness; for he still supposes, because he is a fierce fire-source, that he is higher than humility, seeing that he can sweep along in a terrible manner. But because he must not touch the virgin twig, he makes use of nothing but guile and villainy, and covers the twig, that it may not be known in this world; otherwise there might grow too many such twigs for him in his so-called country, for he is hostile to them. He brings his proud servants with mockery and molestation upon any such man, so that he is persecuted, derided and accounted a fool. This he does by the reason-wise world, by those who call themselves shepherds of Christ, whom the world has regard to, in order that the lily-twig may not be known; otherwise men might observe it, and for him there might grow too many such twigs, and hence he might lose his dominion among men.

8. But the noble lily-twig grows in patience and meekness, and receives its essence, power and aroma from the field of God, that is, from the incarnation of Christ. Christ's spirit is its power, God's essence is its body. Not from a foreign property, but from its own essence which is shut up in death and budding forth in Christ's spirit does the virgin lily-twig grow. It seeks not nor desires the beauty of this world, but of the angelic world; for it grows not in this world, in the third Principle, but in the second Principle, in the paradisaical world. Therefore there is great strife in flesh and blood, in the outer reason. The old Adam knows not the new and yet finds that he resists him: the new one wills not what the old Adam wills, he is always leading the latter to abstinence. This afflicts the old Adam, who desires only pleasure, possessions and temporal honour, and cannot suffer mockery and tribulation. But the new Adam is well pleased to bear the marks of Christ, that he may become like the image of Christ. Therefore the old Adam goes about often mournfully, for he sees that he must be regarded as a fool; nor knows what is happening to him, for he knows not God's will, he has only the will of this world: what shines there he will have, he would fain always be master, before whom people bow. But the new Adam bows himself before his God; he desires nothing, wills nothing, but only longs after his God as a child after its mother; he casts himself into the bosom of his mother and gives himself up to his heavenly mother in the spirit of Christ; he desires of his eternal mother food and drink, and eats in the bosom of the mother as a child in the womb eats of its mother. For as long as he is covered up in the old Adam, he is still in process of incarnation; but when the old Adam dies, the new Adam is born from the old he abandons the vessel, in which he lay and became a virgin child, to the earth and to the judgment of God; but

he is born as a flower in God's kingdom. Then when the day of restoration shall come, all his works, which he has done in the old Adam, shall follow him; the iniquity of the old Adam, however, shall be burnt away in the fire of God and given to the devil for food.

9. Here Reason says: Since then the new man in this world, in the old Adam, is only in process of incarnation, he is not perfect. Answer: This is no otherwise than as in a child, the seed being sown with two tinctures, masculine and feminine, united in each other, and from it a child grows. For as soon as a man turns round, and turns himself to God with his whole heart, mind and will, and goes out from the godless way and gives himself up in real earnest to God, then the gestation begins in the soul's fire, in the old corrupt image, and the soul seizes in itself the Word which put itself in motion in Mary in the centre of the Holy Trinity, which gave itself to Mary, to the half-dead virgin, with the chaste highly blessed heavenly Virgin of the wisdom of God, and became a true man. This Word, which moved or stirred itself in Mary in the centre of the Holy Trinity, which espoused itself with the half-dead shut-up virginity, is laid hold of by the soul's fire, and gestation begins immediately in the soul's image, that is, in the soul's light in the gentleness, in the shut-up virgin essence. For man's love-tincture seizes God's love-tincture, and the seed is sown in the Holy Spirit in the soul's image.

10. Now consider: When the virgin sign presents itself thus in God's love, such a twig may indeed be born, for in God all is perfect. But as long as it is covered up in the old Adam, and stands as it were in essence only as a seed, there is yet great danger in connection with it, for many a one attains this twig only at his latter end; and though he had brought it with him out of the womb, it yet becomes

deteriorated and in the case of some is broken and terrestrialized.

11. So is it likewise with the poor sinner. When he repents, but afterwards becomes again a bad man, it fares with him as befell Adam, who was a beautiful, glorious image, created by God and highly enlightened; but when he let himself be overcome by desire, he became earthly and his beautiful image was imprisoned in the earthly source in the wrath of God: and so it happens still. But this we say, as having received illumination in the grace of God and having striven a considerable time for this garland, that to him who continues steadfast in real earnest, until his twig becomes a tree, his twig in one or more storms will not easily be broken; for what is feeble has also a feeble life. We do not thus break in upon the Deity. On the contrary, the position is of a natural kind, and indeed all comes to pass naturally; for the Eternal itself has also its nature, and one merely proceeds out of another. If this world had not been poisoned by the malice and wrath of the devil, Adam would have remained in this world in Paradise, nor would there have been any such wrath in the stars and elements; for the devil was a king and great lord in the place of this world: he has stirred up the wrath. God therefore created the heaven out of the midst of the waters in order that the fiery nature, viz. the fiery firmament, might be subject to the watery heaven, that its wrath might be extinguished. Otherwise, if the water were to disappear, we should certainly see what there would be in this world, namely, nothing but a mere cold, sour, fiery burning, and yet wholly dark, for there could be no light, because light exists only in the gentleness; hence also there can be no shining fire, unless it have gentle essentiality. And we can recognize that God has transmuted the heavenly essentiality into water, which

was done naturally when God the Father put himself in motion and the devil fell, who wished to be a fire-lord over the gentleness; thus, such a bar was placed before his poisonous malignity that he is now God's ape and not lord, a rager and fulfiller in the wrathful source.

12. Seeing then we know that we are surrounded by the wrath, we ought to take heed to ourselves and not estimate ourselves lightly; for we have our being not only from this world, but also from the divine world, which lies hidden in this world and is near us. We may live and be at the same time in three worlds, if we bud forth again out of the evil life with the virgin image. For we live: (1) in the first Principle in the Father's world in fire, according to the essential soul, that is, according to the fire-source in the centre of nature of eternity; and (2) with the true pure virgin image we live in the light-flaming paradisaical world, although it is not manifest in the place of this world, but yet is known in the virgin image in the Holy Spirit, and in the Word which dwells in the virgin image; and (3) we live with the old Adam in this external corrupt distempered world, along with the devil in his enkindled desire: therefore it is necessary to be cautious. Christ says: *Be simple as doves and wise as serpents* (Matt. 10:16). Take heed to yourselves. In God's kingdom we need no guile, we are only children in the bosom of the mother; but in this world we should certainly be on our guard, we carry the noble treasure in an earthly vessel. It is soon done, losing God and the kingdom of heaven, which after this time can no longer be attained. Here, we are in the field and as seed, we are here in process of growth; though the stalk be broken, the root is still present, so that another stalk may grow.

13. In this life the door of grace stands open to man. However great the sinner, if he turn round and produce

honest fruits of repentance, he may be newborn out of what is bad. But he who deliberately casts his root into the devil's fire (corruption) and despairs of his budding forth: who shall help him, who himself wills not? But if he turn his will to God, then God will have him. For he who wills into God's wrath, him will God's wrath have; but he who wills into the love, him will God's love have. Paul says: *To whom ye yield yourselves servants to obey, his servants ye are to whom ye obey; whether of sin unto death, or of obedience unto righteousness* (Rom. 6:16). The wicked man is to God a sweet savour in the wrath, and the holy man is to God a sweet savour in His love (2 Cor. 2:15-16). A man can make of himself what he pleases: he has the two before him, viz. fire and light. If he will be an angel in the light, then the Spirit of God in Christ helps him to enter the angelic host; if he will be a devil in the fire, then God's anger and wrath help him, and draw him into the abyss to the devil. Further, he gets his ascendant, of which he has desire. But if he break the first desire and enter into another, then he gets another ascendant; but the first clings to him strongly, it strives continually to possess him again. Therefore the noble grain must frequently be in a great strait; it must suffer itself to be pricked by thorns, for the serpent always stings the woman's seed, that is, the child of the virgin, in the heel. The sting of the serpent lies in the old Adam, it always stings the child of the virgin in the mother's womb, in the heel. Therefore life in this world is with us poor imprisoned men a vale of sorrow, full of anxiety, tribulation, misery and affliction. We are here strange guests, and are upon our pilgrim's path. We must traverse great waste, wild solitudes, and are surrounded with evil beasts, with adders and serpents, wolves and nothing but horrible beasts, and the most evil beast we carry in our bosom. In this evil villainous stable our fair virgin lodges.

14. But this we know and with good reason say, that when the noble twig grows and becomes strong, there in that man must the old Adam become servant, he must walk behind, and often do what he does not wish. Often, he must suffer tribulation, mockery and even death. This he does not do willingly, but the virgin image in Christ constrains him; for it would follow joyfully after Christ, who is its bridegroom, and become like Him in tribulation and affliction.

15. And certainly no one is crowned with the virgin's crown which the woman in the Revelation of John wears with twelve stars, viz. with six spirits of nature of a heavenly kind, and with six spirits of an earthly kind, unless he stand firm against the torrent of the dragon and flee into Egypt, that is, under the cross into the plagues of Egypt. He must carry the cross of Christ and put on Christ's crown of thorns, suffer himself to be mocked, fooled and scorned, if he would put on the crown of Christ and of the virgin. He must first wear the crown of thorns, if he would put on the heavenly crown of pearls in the *Ternarius Sanctus*.

16. And we make known to the illuminates another great mystery, namely, that when the pearl is sown, the soul for the first time puts on the crown in the *Ternarius Sanctus* with great joy and honour before God's angels and all the holy virgins. And there is assuredly great joy there, for in that place God becomes man. But this crown conceals itself again. How should there not be joy there? The old Adam dances also, but as an ass to the sound of the lyre; but the crown is assigned to the incarnation.

17. Wouldest thou be a champion, then thou must in Christ's footsteps wage war with the old ass, as well as fight against the devil. If thou conquer and art

acknowledged and accepted as a valiant child of God, the woman's crown with twelve stars will be put on thee. That shalt thou wear, till the virgin be born out of the woman from thy death or by thy death; she shall put on the triple crown of great honour in the *Ternarius Sanctus*. For as long as the virgin image is still shut up in the old Adam, it attains not the angelic crown, as it is still in danger. But when it is born at the death of the old Adam and emerges from the husk or shell, then it is an angel and can no longer perish, and the right crown as assigned, in which God became man, is put upon it. But the crown with the twelve stars it retains as an eternal sign; for it must never be forgotten that God has in the earthly woman again disclosed the virginity and become man. The Deity is spirit, and the holy pure Element is born out of the Word of eternity; and the master has passed into servant, at which all the angels in heaven marvel: and it is the greatest wonder which has been done from eternity, for it is against nature, and such may be described as love. The six earthly signs of the crown with twelve stars shall stand as an eternal wonder and be an eternal song of praise, in that God has redeemed us out of death and distress; and the six heavenly signs shall be our crown and glory, to show that we have overcome what is earthly by what is heavenly, that we were men and women, and thereafter are chaste virgins filled with love proper. Thus the signs of victory shall continue to eternity, whereby shall be recognized what God has had to do with humanity, and how man is the greatest wonder in heaven, at which the angels highly rejoice.

V. OF THE SUPRASENSUAL LIFE

THE SUPRASENSUAL LIFE

"We speak the hidden mystical wisdom of God, which God ordained before the world unto our glory: Which none of the princes of this world knew: For had they known it, they would not have crucified the Lord of glory. But, as it is written, Eye hath not seen, nor ear heard, neither hath it entered into the heart of man to conceive the things which God hath prepared for them that love him. But God hath revealed them unto us by his spirit: For the Spirit searcheth all things, yea, the deep things of God. For what man knoweth the things of a man, save the spirit of a man, which is in him? Even so the things of God knoweth no man, but the spirit of God. Now we have received, not the spirit of the world, but the spirit which is of God; that we might know the things that are freely given us of God. Which things also we speak, not in the words which man's wisdom teacheth, but which the Holy Ghost teacheth; comparing spiritual things with spiritual. But the natural man receiveth not the things of the Spirit of God: For they are foolishness unto him; neither can he know them, because they are spiritually discerned. But he that is spiritual judgeth, or discerneth all things." -

1 Corinthians 2:7-15

The Disciple said to the Master: Master, how may I come to the Suprasensual Life, so that I may see God, and hear God speak?

The Master answered and said: When you can throw yourself into That, where no Creature dwells, if only for a Moment, then you will hear God speak.

Disciple. Is that place where no Creature dwells near at hand; or is it far off?

Master. *It is in you.* And if you can, for a time, cease from all your own thinking and willing, then you will hear the unspeakable Words of God.

Disciple. How can I hear Him speak, when I stand still from thinking and willing?

Master. When you stand still from the thinking of Self, and the willing of Self; when both your intellect and will are quiet, and passive to the Expressions of the Eternal Word and Spirit; and when your Soul is winged up, and above that which is temporal, the outward Senses, and the Imagination being locked up by holy Abstraction, then the Eternal Hearing, Seeing, and Speaking will be revealed in you; and so God hears and sees through you, being now the Organ of His Spirit; and so God speaks in you, and whispers to your Spirit, and your Spirit hears His Voice. Blessed are you therefore if you can stand still from Self-thinking and Self-willing, and can stop the Wheel of your Imagination and Senses; for thus you may arrive at length to see the great Salvation of God being made capable of all Manner of Divine Sensations and Heavenly Communications. Since it is nothing but your own Hearing and Willing that hinder you, so that you do not see and hear God.

Disciple. With what shall I hear and see God, since He is above Nature and Creature?

Master. When you are quiet and silent, then you are as God was before Nature and Creature; you are what God then was; you are that from which He made your Nature and Creature: then you hear and see with that by which God Himself saw and heard in you, even before your own Willing or your own Seeing began.

Disciple. What now hinders or keeps me back, so that I cannot come to that, wherewith God is to be seen and heard?

Master. Your own Willing, Hearing, and Seeing keep you back from it, and hinder you from coming to the Suprasensual State. And it is because you strive against that, out of which you yourself are descended and derived, that you separate yourself, with your own Willing, from God's Willing, and with your own Seeing, from God's Seeing. In your own Seeing you see in your own Willing only, and with your own Understanding you understand in and according to your own Willing, which is divided from the Divine Will. Your Willing moreover stops your Hearing, and makes you deaf towards God, through your own thinking upon terrestrial Things, and your attending to that which is outside you; and so it brings you into a Ground, where you are laid hold on and captivated in Nature. And having brought you here, it overshadows you with that which you will; it binds you with your own Chains, and it keeps you in your own dark Prison which you make for yourself; so that you cannot go out thence, or come to that State which is Supernatural and Suprasensual.

Disciple. But since I am in Nature, and bound with my own Chains, and by my own natural Will; be so kind as to tell me how I may come through Nature into the

Suprasensual and Supernatural Ground, without destroying Nature?

Master. Three Things are requisite in order to this. The *First* is, You must surrender up your Will to God; and must sink yourself down to the Dust in His Mercy. The *Second* is, You must hate your own Will, and forbear from doing that to which your own Will drives you. The *Third* is, You must bow your soul under the Cross, heartily submitting yourself to it, that you may be able to bear the Temptations of Nature and Creature. And if you do thus, God will speak into you, and will bring your surrendered Will into Himself, in the Supernatural Ground; and then you shall hear what the Lord speaks in you.

Disciple. This is a hard saying, Master, for I must forsake the World, and my Life too, if I should do thus.

Master. Be not discouraged at this. If you forsake the World, then you come into that out of which the World is made; and if you lose your Life, then your Life is in that, for whose sake you forsake it. Your Life is in God, from whence it came into the Body; and as you come to have your own Power faint and weak and dying, the Power of God will then work in you and through you.

Disciple. Nevertheless as God has created Man in and for the Natural Life, to rule over all Creatures on Earth, and to be a Lord over all Things in this World, it seems not to be at all unreasonable, that Man should therefore possess this World, and the Things therein for his own.

Master. If you rule over all creatures outwardly, there cannot be much in that. But if you have a Mind to possess all Things and to be a Lord indeed over all Things in this World, there is quite another Method to be taken by you.

Disciple. Pray, how is that? And what Method must I take to arrive at this Sovereignty?

Master. You must learn to distinguish well betwixt the Thing, and that which only is an image thereof; betwixt that Sovereignty which is substantial, and in the inward Ground or Nature, and that which is imaginary, and in an outward Form, or Semblance; betwixt that which is properly Angelical, and that which is no more than bestial. If you rule now over the Creatures externally only, and not from the right internal Ground of the renewed Nature; then your Will and ruling is verily in a bestial Kind or Manner, and yours is at best but a Sort of imaginary and transitory Government, being void of that which is substantial and permanent, which you are to desire and press after. Thus by your outwardly lording it over the Creatures, it is most easy for you to lose the Substance and the Reality, while you have nothing remaining but the Image or Shadow only of your first and original Lordship; wherein you are made capable to be again invested, if you are wise, and take your Investiture from the Supreme Lord in the right Course and Manner. Whereas by your willing and ruling thus after a bestial Manner, you bring also your Desire into a bestial Essence, by which Means you become infected and captivated therein, and get with it a bestial Nature and Condition of Life. But if you shall have put off the bestial and feral Nature, and if you have left the imaginary Life, and quitted the low imaged Condition of it; then you are come into the super-imaginal consciousness, and into the intellectual Life, which is a State of living above Images, Figures, and Shadows, And so you rule over all Creatures, being reunited with your Original, in that very Ground or Source, out of which they were and are created; and henceforth nothing on Earth can hurt you. For you are like all things: and nothing is unlike you.

Disciple. Master, pray teach me how I may come the shortest Way to be like unto All Things.

Master. Just think on the Words of our Lord Jesus Christ; when He said, *"Except you be converted, and become as little Children, you shall not enter into the Kingdom of Heaven."* There is no shorter Way than this; neither can there be a better Way found. Verily, Jesus says unto you, *Unless you turn and become as a Child, hanging upon Him for All Things, you shall not see the Kingdom of God.* Do this, and nothing shall hurt you; for you shall be in Friendship with all Things, as you depend on the Author and Fountain of them all, and become like Him, by such Dependence, and by the Union of your Will with His Will.

But mark what I have further to say; and do not be startled at it, though it may seem hard for you at first to conceive. If you will be like All Things, you must forsake All Things; you must turn your Desire away from them All, and not desire or hanker after any of them; you must not extend your Will to possess that for your own, or as your own, which is Something, whatsoever that Something be. For as soon as ever you take Something into your Desire, and receive it into you for your own, or in Propriety, then this very Something (of whatever Nature it is) is the same with yourself; and this works with you in your Will, and you are thence bound to protect it, and to take Care of it even as of your own Being. But if you receive no Thing into your Desire, then you are free from All Things, and rule over all Things at once, as a Prince of God. For you have received nothing for your own, and are nothing to all Things; and all Things are as nothing to you. You are as a

Child, which understands not what a Thing is; and though you do perhaps understand it, yet you understand it without mixing with it, and without sensibly affecting or touching your Perception, even in that Manner wherein God does rule and see all Things; He comprehending All, and yet nothing comprehending Him.

Disciple. Ah! How shall I arrive at this Heavenly Understanding, at this Sight of All Things in God, at this pure and naked Knowledge which is abstracted from the Senses; at this Light above Nature and Creature; and at this Participation of the Divine Wisdom which oversees all Things, and governs through all intellectual Beings? For, alas, I am touched every Moment by the Things which are about me; and overshadowed by the Clouds and Fumes which rise up out of the Earth. I desire therefore to be taught, if possible, how I may attain such a State and Condition that no Creature may be able to touch me to hurt me; and how my Mind, being purged from sensible Objects and Things, may be prepared for the Entrance and Habitation of the Divine Wisdom in me?

Master. You desire that I would teach you how you are to attain it; and I will direct you to our Master, from Whom I have been taught it, that you may learn it yourself from Him, Who alone teaches the Heart. Hear Him. Would you arrive at this; would you remain untouched by the Sensory; would you behold Light in the very Light of God, and see all Things thereby; then consider the Words of Christ, Who is that Light, and Who is the Truth. O consider now His Words, who said, *"Without Me you can do nothing,"* and do not hesitate to apply yourself unto Him, Who is the Strength of your Salvation, and the Power of your Life; and with Whom you can do all Things, by the Faith which He works in you. But unless you wholly give yourself up to the Life of our Lord Jesus

Christ, and surrender your Will wholly to Him, and desire nothing without Him, you shall never come to that Rest that no Creature can disturb. Think what you please, and delight in the Activity of your own Reason, but you shall find that in your own Power, and without such a total Surrender to God, and to the Life of God, you can never arrive at such a Rest as this, or the true Quiet of the Soul, wherein no Creature can molest you, or so much as touch you. Which when you shall, by Grace, have attained to, then with your Body you are in the World, as in the properties of outward Nature; and with your Reason, under the Cross of our Lord Jesus Christ; but with your Will you walk in Heaven, and are at the End from whence all Creatures are proceeded forth, and to which they return again. And then you can in this End, which is the same with the Beginning, behold all Things outwardly with the Reason, and inwardly with the Mind; and so may you rule in all Things and over all Things, with Christ; unto whom all Power is given both in Heaven and on Earth.

Disciple. O Master, the Creatures which live in me do withhold me, so that I cannot so wholly yield and give up myself as I willingly would. What am I to do in this case?

Master. Do not let this trouble you. Does your Will go forth from the Creatures? Then the Creatures are forsaken in you. They are in the World; and your Body, which is in the World, is with the Creatures. But spiritually you walk with God, and converse in Heaven; being in your Mind redeemed from Earth, and separated from Creatures, to live the Life of God. And if your Will thus leaves the Creatures, and goes forth from them, even as the Spirit goes forth from the Body at Death; then are the Creatures dead in it, and live only in the Body in the World. Since if your Will does not bring itself into them, they cannot bring themselves into it, neither can they by any Means touch the Soul. And hence St. Paul says, *"Our Conversation is in Heaven";* and also, *"You are the Temple of God, and the Spirit of God dwells in you."* So then true Christians are the very Temples of the Holy Ghost, who dwells in them; that is, the Holy Ghost dwells in the Will, and the Creature dwells in the Body.

Disciple. If now the Holy Spirit dwells in the Will of the Mind, how ought I to keep myself so that He departs not from me again?

Master. Mark the Words of our Lord Jesus Christ: *"If you abide in My Words, then My Words abide in you."* If you abide with your Will, in the Words of Christ; then His Word and Spirit abides in you, and all shall be done for you that you can ask of Him. But if your Will goes into the Creature, then you have broken yourself off from Him; and then you cannot any otherwise keep yourself but by abiding continually in the most surrendered Humility, and by entering into a constant Course of Penitence, wherein you will be always grieved at your own creaturely, and that Creatures do live still in you, that is, in your bodily Appetite. If you do thus, you stand in a daily dying from the Creatures, and in a daily ascending into Heaven in your Will; which Will is also the Will of your Heavenly Father.

Disciple. O my loving Master, pray teach me how I may come to such a constant Course of holy Penitence, and to such a daily dying from all creaturely Objects; for how can I abide continually in Repentance?

Master. When you leave that which loves you, and love that which hates you; then you may abide continually in Repentance.

Disciple. What is it that I must thus leave?

Master. All Things that love and entertain you, because your Will loves and entertains them. All Things that please and feed you, because your Will feeds and cherishes them: All Creatures in Flesh and Blood; in a Word, all Visibles and Sensibles, by which either the Imagination or sensitive Appetite in Men are delighted and refreshed. These the Will of your Mind, or your supreme Part, must leave and forsake; and must even account them all its Enemies. This is the leaving of what loves you. And the loving of what hates you, is the embracing the Reproach of the World. You must learn then to love the Cross of the Lord Jesus Christ, and for His sake to be pleased with the Reproach of the World which hates you and derides you; and let this be your daily Exercise of Penitence to be crucified to the World, and the World to you. And so you shall have continual Cause to hate yourself in the Creature, and to seek the Eternal Rest, which is in Christ. To which Rest you having thus attained, your Will may therein safely rest and repose itself, according as your Lord Christ has said; *"In Me you may have Rest, but in the World you shall have Anxiety: In Me you may have Peace, but in the World you shall have Tribulation."*

Disciple. How shall I be now able to subsist in this Anxiety and Tribulation arising from the World, so as not to lose the Eternal Peace, or not enter into this Rest? And how may I recover myself in such a Temptation as this is, by not sinking under the World, but rising above it by a Life that is truly heavenly and Suprasensual?

Master. If you do once every Hour throw yourself by Faith beyond all Creatures, beyond and above all sensual Perception and Apprehension, yea, above Discourse and Reasoning into the abyssal Mercy of God, into the Sufferings of our Lord, and into the Fellowship of His intercession, and yield yourself fully and absolutely thereinto; then you shall receive Power from above to rule over Death, and the Devil, and to subdue Hell and the World under you: And then you may subsist in all Temptations, and be the brighter for them.

Disciple. Blessed is the Man that arrives to such a State as this. But, alas! Poor Creature that I am, how is this possible as to me? And what, O my Master, would become of me, if I should never attain with my Mind to that, where no Creature is? Must I not cry out, I am undone?

Master. Why are you so dispirited? Be of good Heart still; for you may certainly yet attain to it. Only believe, and all Things are made possible to you. If it were that your Will, O you of little Courage, could break off itself for one Hour, or even but for one half Hour, from all Creatures, and plunge itself into That where no Creature is, or can be, presently it would be penetrated and clothed upon with the greatest Radiance of the Glory of God, would taste in itself the most sweet Love of Jesus, the Sweetness whereof no Tongue can express, and would find in itself the unspeakable Words of our Lord concerning His Great Mercy. Your Spirit would then feel in itself the Cross of our Lord Jesus Christ to be very pleasing: and would thereupon love the Cross more than the Honors and Goods of the World.

Disciple. This would indeed be good for the Soul, but what would become of the Body, seeing that it must live in the Creature?

Master. The Body would by this Means be put into the Imitation of our Lord Christ, and of His Body: It would stand in the Communion of that most Blessed Body, which was the true Temple of the Deity; and in the

Participation of all its gracious Effects, Virtues and Influences. It would live in the Creature not of Choice, but only as it is made subject unto Vanity, and in the World, as it is placed therein by the Ordination of the Creator, for its Cultivation and higher Advancement; and as groaning to be delivered out of it in God's Time and Manner, for its Perfection and Resuscitation in Eternal Liberty and Glory, like unto the Glorified Body of our Lord and His risen Saints.

Disciple. But the Body being in its present Constitution, subject to Vanity, and living in a vain Image and creaturely Shadow, according to the Life of the Creatures or Brutes, whose Breath goes downward to the Earth; I am still very afraid, lest it should continue to depress the Mind which is lifted up to God, by hanging on as a dead Weight; and go on to bemuse and perplex the Mind, as formerly, with Dreams and Trifles, by letting in the Objects from without, in order to draw me down into the Bustling of the World; whereas I would rather maintain my Conversation in Heaven, even while I am living in the World. What therefore must I do with this Body, so that I may be able to keep up so desirable a Conversation; and not to be under any Subjection to it any longer?

Master. There is no other Way for you that I know but to present the Body whereof you complain (which is the Beast to be sacrificed), *"a living sacrifice, holy and acceptable unto God."* And this shall be your rational service, whereby your Body will be put, as you desire, into the Imitation of Jesus Christ, Who said, *His Kingdom was not of this World.* Do not be conformed to it, then, but be transformed by the renewing of your Mind; which renewed Mind is to have Dominion over the Body, so that you may prove, both in Body and Mind, what is the perfect Will of God, and accordingly perform His Will by

His Grace operating in you. Whereupon the Body, or the Animal Life, would, being thus offered up, begin to die, both from without and from within. From without, that is, from the Vanity and evil Customs and Fashions of the World. It would be an utter Enemy to all worldly Pomp, and to all the Foppery, Pageantry, Pride, Ambition, and Haughtiness therein. From within, it would die to all the Lusts and Appetites of the Flesh, and would get a Mind and Will wholly new, for its Government and Management; being now made subject to the Spirit, which would continually be directed to God, and so consequently that which is subject to it, and thus your very Body is become the Temple of God and of His Spirit, in Imitation of your Lord's Body.

Disciple. But the World would hate it, and despise it for so doing; seeing it must hereby contradict the World, and must live and act quite otherwise than the World does. This is most certain. And how can this then be taken?

Master. It would not take that as any Harm done to it, but would rather rejoice that it is become worthy to be like unto the Image of our Lord Jesus Christ, being transformed from that of the World: And it would be most willing to bear that Cross after our Lord; merely that our Lord might bestow upon it the Influence of His sweet and Precious Love.

Disciple. I do not doubt but in some this may be even so. Nevertheless for my own Part, I am in a Straight betwixt two, not feeling yet enough of that blessed Influence upon me. O how willingly should my Body bear that, could this be safely depended upon by me, according to what is urged! Wherefore pardon me, in this one Thing, if my Impatience does still further demand "what would become of it, if the Anger of God from within, and the wicked World also from without, should at once assault it, as the same really happened to our Lord Christ?"

Master. Be that unto you, even as unto our Lord Christ, when He was reproached, reviled and crucified by the World; and when the Anger of God so fiercely assaulted Him for our Sake. Now what did He under this most terrible Assault both from without and from within? Why: He commended His Soul into the Hands of His Father, and so departed from the Anguish of this World into the Eternal Joy. Do you likewise; and His Death shall be your Life.

Disciple. Be it unto me as unto the Lord Christ; and unto my Body as unto His; which into His Hands I have commended, and for the Sake of His Name do offer up, according to His revealed Will. Nevertheless I am desirous to know what would become of my Body in its pressing forth from the Anguish of this miserable World into the Power of the Heavenly Kingdom.

Master. It would get forth from the Reproach and Contradiction of the World, by a Conformity to the Passion of Jesus Christ; and from the Sorrows and Pains in the Flesh, which are only the Effects of some tangible Impression of Things without, by a quiet Introversion of the Spirit, and secret Communion with the Deity manifesting itself for that End. It would penetrate into itself; it would sink into the great Love of God; it would be sustained and refreshed by the most sweet Name Jesus; and it would see and find within itself a new World springing forth as through the Anger of God, into the Love and Joy Eternal. And then should a Man wrap his Soul in this, even in the great Love of God, and clothe himself therewith as with a Garment; and should account thence all Things alike; because in the Creature he finds nothing that can give him without God, the least Satisfaction; and because also nothing of Harm can touch him anymore, while he remains in this Love, the which indeed is stronger than all Things, and makes a Man hence invulnerable both from within and without, by taking out the Sting and Poison of the Creatures, and destroying the Power of Death. And whether the Body is in Hell or on Earth, all is alike to him; for whether it be there or here, his mind is still in the greatest Love of God; which is no less than to say, that he is in Heaven.

Disciple. But how would a Man's Body be maintained in the World; or how would he be able to maintain those that are his, if he should by such a Conversation incur the Displeasure of all the World?

Master. Such a Man gets greater Favors than the World is able to bestow upon him. He has God for his Friend; he has all His Angels for his Friends: In all Dangers and necessities these protect and relieve him; so that he need fear no Manner of Evil; no Creature can hurt him. God is his Helper; and that is sufficient. Also God is his Blessing in every Thing: and though sometimes it may seem as if God would not bless him, yet is this but for a Trial to him, and for the Attraction of the Divine Love; to the End he may more fervently pray to God, and commit all his ways unto Him.

Disciple. He loses however all his good Friends; and there will be none to help him in his Necessity.

Master. Nay, but he gets the Hearts of all his good Friends into his Possession, and loses none but his Enemies, who before loved his Vanity and Wickedness.

Disciple. How is it that he can get his good Friends in his Possession?

Master. He gets the very Hearts and Souls of all those who belong to our Lord Jesus to be his Brethren, and the Members of his own very Life. For all the Children of God are but One in Christ, which one is Christ in All: and therefore He gets them all to be his Fellow Members in the Body of Christ, whence they have all the same Love of God, as the Branches of a Tree in one and the same Root, and spring all from one and the same Source of Life in them. So that he can have no Want of Spiritual Friends and Relations, who are all rooted with him together in the Love which is from above; who are all of the same Blood and Kindred in Christ Jesus; and who are cherished all by the same quickening Sap and Spirit diffusing itself through them universally from the one true Vine, which is the Tree of Life and Love. These are Friends worth having; and though here they may be unknown to him, will abide his Friends beyond Death, to all Eternity. But neither can he want even outward natural Friends; as our Lord Christ when on Earth did not want such also. For though indeed the High-Priests and Potentates of the World could not have a Love to Him, because they belonged not to Him, neither stood in any Kind of Relation to Him, as being not of this World, yet those loved Him who were capable of His Love, and receptive to His Words. So in like Manner, those who love Truth and Righteousness will love that man, and will associate themselves unto him, yea, though they may perhaps be outwardly at some Distance or seeming Disagreement, from the Situation of their worldly Affairs, or out of some certain Respects; yet in their Hearts they cannot but cleave to him. For though they be not yet actually incorporated into one Body with him, yet they cannot resist being of one Mind with him, and being united in Affection for the great Regard they bear to the Truth, which shines forth in his Words and in his Life. By which they are made either his declared or his secret Friends; and he does so get their Hearts, as they will be delighted above all Things in his Company, for the Sake thereof, and will court his Friendship, and will come unto him by Stealth, if openly they dare not, for the Benefit of his Conversation and Advice even as Nicodemus did unto Christ, who came to Him by Night, and in his Heart loved Jesus for the Truth's Sake, though outwardly he feared the World. And thus you shall have many Friends that are not known to you; and some known to you, who may not appear so before the World.

Disciple. Nevertheless it is very grievous to be generally despised of the World, and to be trampled upon by men as the very Offscouring thereof.

Master. That which now seems so hard and heavy to you, you will yet hereafter be most of all in Love with.

Disciple. Loving Master, I am well content that this Love should rule in me over the natural Life, so that I may attain to that which is Supernatural and Suprasensual; but pray tell me now, why must Love and Hatred, Friend and Foe, thus be together? Would not Love alone be better? Wherefore, I say, are Love and Trouble thus joined?

Master. If Love dwelt not in Trouble, it could have nothing to love: but its Substance which it loves, namely, the poor Soul, being in Trouble and Pain, it has thence Cause to love this its own Substance, and to deliver it from Pain; that so itself may be by it again beloved. Neither could anyone know what Love is, if there were no Hatred; or what Friendship is, if there were no Foe to contend with: Or in one Word, if Love had not something which it might love, and manifest the Virtue and Power of Love, by working our Deliverance to the Beloved from all Pain and Trouble.

Disciple. Pray what is the Virtue, the Power, the Height and the Greatness of Love?

Master. The Virtue of Love is Nothing and All, or that Nothing visible out of which All Things proceed; its Power is through All Things; its Height is as high as God; its Greatness is as great as God. Its Virtue is the Principle of all Principles; its Power supports the Heavens and upholds the Earth; its Height is higher than the Highest Heavens; and its Greatness is even greater than the very Manifestation of the Godhead in the glorious Light of the Divine Essence, as being infinitely capable of greater and greater Manifestations in all Eternity. What can I say more? Love is higher than the Highest. Love is greater that the Greatest. Yea, it is in a certain Sense greater than God; while yet in the highest Sense of all, God is Love, and Love is God. Love being the highest Principle, is the Virtue of all Virtues; from whence they flow forth. Love being the greatest Majesty, is the Power of all Powers, from whence they severally operate: And it is the Holy Magical Root, or Ghostly Power from whence all the Wonders of God have been wrought by the Hands of His elect Servants, in all their Generations successively. Whosoever finds it, finds Nothing and All Things.

Disciple. Dear Master, pray tell me how I may understand this.

Master. First then, in that I said, *its Virtue is Nothing,* or *that Nothing,* which is the Beginning of All Things, you must understand it thus: When you are gone forth wholly from the Creature, and from that which is visible, and are become Nothing to all that is Nature and Creature, then you are in that Eternal One, which is God Himself: And then you shall perceive and feel in your Interior, the highest Virtue of Love. But in that I said, *Its Power is* *through All Things*, this is that which you perceive and find in your own Soul and Body experientially, whenever this great Love is enkindled within you; seeing that it will burn more than the Fire can do, as it did in the Prophets of old, and afterwards in the Apostles, when God conversed with them bodily, and when His Spirit descended upon them in the Oratory of Zion. You shall then see also in all the Works of God, how Love has poured forth itself into all Things: Inwardly in the Virtue and Power of every Thing; and outwardly in the Figure and Form thereof.

And in that I said, *Its Height is as high as God*; you may understand this in yourself; forasmuch as it brings you to be as high as God Himself is, by being united to God: As may be seen by our beloved Lord Christ in our Humanity. Which Humanity Love has brought up into the highest Throne, above all Angelical Principalities and Powers, into the very Power of the Deity itself. But in that I also said, *Its Greatness is as great as God*, you are hereby to understand, that there is a certain Greatness and Latitude of Heart in Love, which is inexpressible; for it enlarges the Soul as wide as the whole Creation of God. And this shall be truly experienced by you, beyond all Words, when the Throne of Love shall be set up in your Heart.

Moreover in that I said, *Its Virtue is the Principle of all Principles*, hereby it is given you to understand, that Love is the principiating Cause of all created beings, both spiritual and corporeal, by Virtue of which the second Causes do move and act occasionally, according to certain Eternal Laws from the Beginning implanted in the very Constitution of Things thus originated. This Virtue which is in Love, is the very Life and Energy of all the Principles of Nature, superior and inferior: It reaches to all Worlds, and to all Manner of Beings in them contained, they being the Workmanship of Divine Love and it the first Mover, and first Moveable both in Heaven above and in the Earth beneath, and in the Water under the Earth. And hence there is given to it the Name of the Lucid Aleph, or Alpha; by which is expressed the Beginning of the Alphabet of Nature, and of the Book of Creation and Providence, or the Divine Archetypal Book, in which is the Light of Wisdom, and the Source of all Lights and Forms.

And in that I said, *Its Power supports the Heavens*; by this you will come to understand, that as the Heavens, visible and invisible, are originated from this great Principle, so are they likewise necessarily sustained by it; and that therefore if this should be but never so little withdrawn, all the Lights, Glories, Beauties, and Forms of the heavenly Worlds, would presently sink into Darkness and Chaos.

And whereas I further said, *that it upholds the Earth*: this will appear to you no less evident than the former, and you shall perceive it in yourself by daily and hourly Experience; forasmuch as the Earth without it, even your own Earth also (that is, your Body) would certainly be without Form and void. By the Power thereof the Earth has been thus long upheld, notwithstanding a foreign usurped Power introduced by the Folly of Sin: And should this but once fail or recede, there could no longer be either Vegetation or Animation upon it; yea, the very Pillars of it be overthrown quite, and the Band of Union, which is that of Attraction or Magnetism, called the Centripetal Power, being broken and dissolved, all must thence run into the utmost Disorder, and falling away as into Shivers, would be dispersed as loose Dust before the Wind.

But in that I said, *Its Height is higher than the highest Heavens*; this you may also understand within yourself: For should you ascend in Spirit through all the Orders of Angels and heavenly Powers, yet the Power of Love still is undeniably superior to them all, and as the Throne of God, Who sits upon the Heaven of Heavens, is higher than the highest of them, even so must Love also be, which fills them all, and comprehends them all.

And whereas I said of the Greatness of Love, *that it is greater than the very Manifestation of the Godhead in the Light of the Divine Essence*; that is also true: For Love enters even into that where the Godhead is not manifested in this glorious Light, and where God may be said not to dwell. And entering thereinto, Love begins to manifest to the Soul the Light of the Godhead: and thus is the Darkness broken through, and the Wonders of the new Creation successively manifested.

Thus shall you be brought to understand really and fundamentally, what is the Virtue and Power of Love, and what the Height and Greatness thereof is; how that it is indeed the Virtue of all Virtues, though it be invisible, and as Nothing in Appearance. Inasmuch as it is the Worker of all Things and a powerful vital Energy passing through all Virtues and Powers natural and Supernatural; and the Power of all Powers, nothing being able to let or obstruct the Omnipotence of Love, or to resist Its invincible penetrating Might, which passes through the whole Creation of God, inspecting and governing all Things.

And in that I said, *It is higher than the highest, and greater than the greatest*; you may hereby perceive as in a Glimpse, the supreme Height and Greatness of Omnipotent Love, which infinitely transcends all that human Sense and Reason can reach to. The highest

Archangels and the Greatest Powers of Heaven, are in Comparison of it, but as Dwarfs. Nothing can be conceived higher and greater in God Himself, by the very highest and greatest of His Creatures. There is such an Infinity in it, as comprehends and surpasses all the Divine Attributes.

But in that it was also said, *Its Greatness is greater than God*; that likewise is very true in the Sense wherein it was spoken. For Love, as I before observed, can there enter where God dwells not, since the most high God dwells not in Darkness, but in the Light; the hellish Darkness being put under His Feet. Thus for Instance, when our beloved Lord Christ was in Hell, Hell was not the Mansion of God or of Christ; Hell was not God, neither was it with God, nor could it be at all with Him; Hell stood in the Darkness and Anxiety of Nature, and no Light of the Divine Majesty did there enter: God was not there; for He is not in the Darkness, or in the Anguish; but Love Was there; and Love destroyed Death and conquered Hell. So also when you are in Anguish or Trouble, which is Hell within God is not the Anguish or Trouble; neither is He in the Anguish or Trouble; but His Love is there, and brings you out of the Anguish and Trouble into God, leading you into the Light and joy of His Presence, When God hides Himself in you, Love is still there, and makes Him manifest in you. Such is the inconceivable Greatness and Largeness of Love; which will hence appear to you as great as God above Nature, and greater than God in Nature, or as considered in His manifestative Glory.

Lastly, Whereas I also said, *Whosoever finds it, finds Nothing and All Things*; that is also certain and true. But how finds he Nothing? Why, I will tell you how. He that finds it, finds a Supernatural Suprasensual Abyss, which has no Ground or Byss to stand on, and where there is no Place to dwell in; and he finds also Nothing is like unto it, and therefore it may fitly be compared to Nothing; for it is deeper than any Thing, and is as Nothing with Respect to All Things, forasmuch as it is not comprehensible by any of them. And because it is Nothing respectively, it is therefore free from All Things; and is that only Good, which a Man cannot express or utter what it is; there being Nothing to which it may be compared, to express it by.

But in that I lastly said, *Whosoever finds it, finds All Things*; there is nothing can be more true than this Assertion. It has been the Beginning of All Things; and it rules All Things. It is also the End of All Things; and will thence comprehend All Things within its Circle. All Things are from it, and in it, and by it. If you find it, you come into that Ground from whence All Things are proceeded, and wherein they subsist; and you are in it a King over all the Works of God.

Here the Disciple was exceedingly ravished with what his Master had so wonderfully and surprisingly declared, and returned his most humble and hearty Thanks for that Light, which he had been an Instrument of conveying to him. But being desirous to hear further concerning these high Matters, and to know somewhat more particularly, he requested him, that he would give him Leave to wait on him the next Day again; and that he would then be pleased to show him how and where he might find this which was so much beyond all Price and Value, and whereabout the Seat and Abode of it might be in human Nature; with the entire Process of the Discovery and bringing it forth to Light.

The Master said to him: This then we will discourse about at our next Conference, as God shall reveal the same to us by His Spirit, which is a Searcher of All Things. And if you do remember well what I answered you in the Beginning, you shall soon come thereby to understand that hidden mystical Wisdom of God, which none of the Wise Men of the World know; and where the Mine thereof is to be found in you, shall be given you from above to discern. Be silent therefore in your Spirit, and watch unto Prayer; that when we meet again Tomorrow in the Love of Christ, your Mind may be disposed for finding that noble Pearl, which to the World appears Nothing, but which to the Children of Wisdom is All Things.

DIALOGUE II

Herein is described and set forth the Manner of passing the Gulf which divides betwixt the two Principles or States of Heaven and Hell: and it is particularly shown how this Transaction is carried on in the Soul; what the Partition Wall therein is, which separates from God.

What the breaking down of this Partition Wall, and how effected; what the Centre of Light is, and the pressing into that Centre is; What the Light of God, and the Light of Nature are; how they are operative in their several Spheres, and how to be kept from interfering with each other; with some Account of the two Wills and their Contraposition in the Fallen State; of the Magical Wheel of the Will, and how the Motion thereof may be regulated; of the Eye in the Midst thereof, what the Right Eye is to the Soul, and what the Left is, but especially what the Single Eye is, and in what Manner it is to be obtained; of Purification from the Contagion of Matter, of the Destruction of Evil, and of the very Annihilation of it, by the Subsidence of the Will from its own Something into Nothing; of the Naked and Magical Faith, and the Attraction thereby of a certain Divine Substantiality and Vestment; how all consists in the Will, and proceeds but from one Point; where that Point is placed, and how it may be found out; and which is both the safest and nearest Way to attain to the high Suprasensual State, and the internal Kingdom of Christ, according to the true Heavenly Magia or Wisdom.

The Disciple being very earnest to be more fully instructed how he might arrive at the Suprasensual Life, and how, having found all Things, he might come to be a king over all God's Works, came again to his Master the next Morning, having watched the Night in Prayer, that he might be disposed to receive and apprehend the Instructions that should be given him by Divine Irradiation upon his Mind. And the Disciple after a little Space of Silence, bowed himself, and thus brake forth:

Disciple. O my Master! My Master! I have now endeavored so to recollect my Soul in the Presence of God, and to cast myself into that Deep where no Creature does nor can dwell; that I might hear the Voice of my Lord speaking in me; and be initiated into that high Life, whereof I heard yesterday such great and amazing Things pronounced. But, alas! I neither hear nor see as I should: There is still such a Partition Wall in me which beats back the Heavenly Sounds in their Passage, and obstructs the Entrance of that Light by which alone Divine Objects are discoverable, as till this be broken down, I can have but small Hopes, yea, even none at all, of arriving at those glorious Attainments which you pressed me to, or of entering into that where no Creature dwells, and which you call Nothing and All Things. Wherefore be so kind as to inform me what is required on my Part, that this Partition which hinders may be broken or removed.

Master. This Partition is the Creaturely Will in you: and this can be broken by nothing but by the Grace of Self-Denial, which is the Entrance into the true following of Christ; and totally removed by nothing but a perfect Conformity with the Divine Will.

Disciple. But how shall I be able to break this Creaturely Will, which is in me, and is at Enmity with the Divine Will? Or, what shall I do to follow Christ in so difficult a Path, and not to faint in a continual Course of Self-Denial and Surrender to the Will of God?

Master. This is not to be done by yourself, but by the Light and Grace of God received into your Soul, which will if you gainsay not, break the Darkness that is in you, and melt down your own Will, which works in the Darkness and Corruption of Nature, and bring it into the Obedience of Christ, whereby the Partition of the Creaturely Self is removed from betwixt God and you.

Disciple. I know that I cannot do it of myself. But I would fain learn how I must receive this Divine Light and Grace into me, which is to do it for me, if I hinder it: not my own Self. What is then required of me in order to admit this Breaker of the Partition and to Promote the Attainment of the Ends of such Admission?

Master. There is nothing more required of you at first, than not to resist this Grace, which is manifested in you, and nothing in the whole Process of your Work, but to be obedient and passive to the Light of God shining through the Darkness of your Creaturely Being, which comprehends it not, as reaching no higher than the Light of Nature.

Disciple. But is it not for me to attain, if I can, both the Light of God, and the Light of the outward Nature too: And to make use of them both for the ordering my Life wisely and prudently?

Master. It is right, I confess, so to do. And it is indeed a Treasure above all earthly Treasures, to be possessed of the Light of God and Nature, operating in their Spheres; and to have both the Eye of Time and Eternity at once open together, and yet not to interfere with each other.

Disciple. This is a great Satisfaction to me to hear; having been very uneasy about it for some Time. But how this can be without interfering with each other, there is the

Difficulty: Wherefore fain would I know, if it were lawful, the Boundaries of the one and the other; and how both the Divine and the Natural Light may in their several Spheres respectively act and operate, for the Manifestation of the Mysteries of God and Nature, and for the Conduct of my outward and inward Life?

Master. That each of these may be preserved distinct in their several Spheres, without confounding Things Heavenly and Things Earthly, or breaking the golden Chain of Wisdom, it will be necessary, my Child, in the first Place to wait for and attend the Supernatural and Divine Light, as that superior Light appointed to govern the Day, rising in the true East, which is the Centre of Paradise; and in great Might breaking forth as out of the Darkness within you, through a Pillar of Fire and Thunder Clouds, and thereby also reflecting upon the inferior Light of Nature a Sort of Image of itself, whereby only it can be kept in its due Subordination, that which is below being made subservient to that which is above; and that which is without to that which is within. Thus there will be no Danger of interfering; but all will go right, and every Thing abide in its proper Sphere.

Disciple. Therefore, unless Reason or the Light of Nature be sanctified in my Soul, and illuminated by this superior Light, as from the central East of the holy Light-World, by the Eternal and Intellectual Sun; I perceive there will be always some Confusion, and I shall never be able to manage aright either what concerns Time or Eternity: But I must always be at a Loss, or break the Links of Wisdom's Chain.

Master. It is even so as you have said. All is Confusion, if you have no more but the dim Light of Nature, or unsanctified and unregenerate Reason to guide you by;

and if only the Eye of Time be opened in you, which cannot pierce beyond its own Limit. Wherefore seek the Fountain of Light, waiting in the deep Ground of your Soul for the rising there of the Sun of Righteousness, whereby the Light of Nature in you, with the Properties thereof, will be made to shine seven Times brighter than ordinary. For it shall receive the Stamp, Image, and Impression of the Suprasensual and Supernatural; so that the sensual and rational Life will hence be brought into the most perfect Order and Harmony.

Disciple. But how am I to wait for the rising of this glorious Sun, and how am I to seek in the Centre, this Fountain of Light, which may enlighten me throughout, and bring all my Properties into perfect Harmony? I am in Nature as I said before; and which Way shall I pass through Nature, and the Light thereof, so that I may come into that Supernatural and Suprasensual Ground, whence this true Light, which is the Light of Minds, does arise; and this, without the Destruction of my Nature, or quenching the Light of it, which is my Reason?

Master. Cease but from your own Activity, steadfastly fixing your eye upon one point, and with a strong purpose relying upon the promised grace of God in Christ, to bring you out of your darkness into His marvelous light. For this end gather in all your thoughts, and by faith press into the Centre, laying hold upon the Word of God, which is infallible, and which has called you. Be you then obedient to this call; and be silent before the Lord, sitting alone with Him in your inmost and most hidden cell, your mind being centrally united in itself, and attending His will in the patience of Hope. So shall your light break forth as the morning; and after the redness thereof is passed, the Sun Himself, which you wait for, shall arise unto you, and under His most healing wings you shall greatly rejoice;

ascending and descending in His bright and salutiferous beams. Behold this is the true Suprasensual ground of life.

Disciple. I believe it indeed to be even so. But will not this destroy Nature? Will not the Light of Nature in me be extinguished by this greater Light? Or, must not the outward Life hence perish with the earthly Body which I carry?

Master. By no Means at all. It is true, the evil Nature will be destroyed by it; but by the Destruction thereof you can be no Loser, but very much a Gainer. The Eternal Band of Nature is the same afterward as before; and the Properties are the same. So that Nature hereby is only advanced and meliorated; and the Light thereof, or human Reason, by being kept within its due Bounds, and regulated by a superior Light, is only made useful.

Disciple. Pray therefore let me know how this inferior Light ought to be used by me how it is to be kept within its due Bounds and after what Manner the superior Light does regulate it and ennoble it.

Master. Know then, my beloved Son, that if you will keep the Light of Nature within its own proper Bounds, and make use thereof in just Subordination to the Light of God: you must consider that there are in the Soul two Wills, an inferior Will, which is for driving you to Things without and below; and a superior Will, which is for drawing to Things within and above. These two Wills are now set together, as it were, Back to Back, and in a direct Contrariety to each other; but in the Beginning it was not so. For this Contraposition of the Soul in these two is no more than the Effect of the Fallen State; since before that they were placed one under the other, that is, the superior Will Above, as the Lord, and the inferior Below, as the Subject. And thus it ought to have continued. You must also further consider, that answering to these two Wills there are likewise two Eyes in the Soul, whereby they are severally directed; forasmuch as these Eyes are not united in one single View, but look quite contrary Ways at once. They are in a like Manner set one against the other, without a common Medium to join them. And hence, so long as this Double-sightedness does remain, it is impossible there should be any Agreement in the Determination of this or that Will. This is very plain: And it shows the Necessity that this Malady, arising from the Disunion of the Rays of Vision be some Way remedied and redressed, in order to a true Discernment in the Mind. Both these Eyes therefore must be made to unite by a Concentration of Rays; there being nothing more dangerous than for the Mind to abide thus in the Duplicity, and not to seek to arrive at the Unity. You perceive, I know, that you have two Wills in you, one set against the other, the superior and the inferior; and that you have also two Eyes within, one against another whereof the one Eye may be called the Right Eye, and the other the Left Eye. You perceive too, doubtless, that it is according to the Right Eye that the Wheel of the superior Will is moved; and that it is according to the Motion of the Left Eye, that the contrary Wheel in the lower is turned about.

Disciple. I perceive this, Sir, to be very true; and this it is which causes a continual Combat in me, and creates to me greater Anxiety than I am able to express. Nor am I unacquainted with the Disease of my own Soul, which you have so clearly declared. Alas! I perceive and lament this Malady, which so miserably disturbs my Sight; whence I feel such irregular and convulsive Motions drawing me on this Side and that Side. The Spirit sees not as the Flesh sees; neither does, or can the Flesh see, as the

Spirit sees. Hence the Spirit wills against the Flesh; and the Flesh wills against the Spirit in me. This has been my hard Case. And how shall it be remedied? O how may I arrive at the Unity of Will, and how come into the Unity of Vision!

Master. Mark now what I say: The Right Eye looks forward in you into Eternity. The Left Eye looks backward in you into Time. If now you suffer yourself to be always looking into Nature, and the Things of Time, and to be leading the Will and to be seeking somewhat for itself in the Desire, it will be impossible for you ever to arrive at the Unity, which you wish for Remember this; and be upon your watch, Give not your Mind leave to enter in, nor to fill itself with, that which is without you: neither look you backward upon yourself; but quit yourself, and look forward upon Christ. Let not your Left Eye deceive you, by making continually one Representation after another, and stirring up thereby an earnest Longing in the Self-Propriety; but let your Right Eye command back this Left, and attract it to you, so that it may not gad abroad into the Wonders and Delights of Nature. Yea, it is better to pluck it quite out, and to cast it from you, than to suffer it to proceed forth without Restraint into Nature, and to follow its own Lusts: However there is for this no necessity, since both Eyes may become very useful, if ordered aright; and both the Divine and natural Light may in the Soul subsist together, and be of mutual Service to each other. But never shall you arrive at the Unity of Vision or Uniformity of Will, but by entering fully into the Will of our Savior Christ, and therein bringing the Eye of Time into the Eye of Eternity; and then descending by Means of this united through the Light of God into the Light of Nature.

Disciple. So then if I can but enter into the Will of my Lord, and abide therein, I am safe, and may both attain to the Light of God in the Spirit of my Soul, and see with the Eye of God, that is, the Eye of Eternity in the Eternal Ground of my Will; and may also at the same Time enjoy the Light of this World nevertheless; not degrading, but adorning the Light of Nature; and beholding as with the Eye of Eternity Things Eternal, so with the Eye of Nature Things natural, and both contemplating therein the Wonders of God, and sustaining also thereby the Life of my outward Vehicle or body.

Master. It is very right. You have well understood; and you desire now to enter into the Will of God, and to abide therein as in the Suprasensual Ground of Light and Life, where you may in His Light behold both Time and Eternity, and bring all the Wonders created of God for the exterior into the interior Life, and so eternally rejoice in them to the Glory of Christ; the Partition of your Creaturely Will being broken down, and the Eye of your Spirit simplified in and through the Eye of God manifesting itself in the Centre of your Life. Let this be so now; for it is God's Will.

Disciple. But it is very hard to be always looking forwards into Eternity; and consequently to attain to this single Eye, and Simplicity of Divine Vision. The Entrance of a Soul naked into the Will of God, shutting out all Imaginations and Desires, and breaking down the strong Partition which you mention, is indeed somewhat very terrible and shocking to human Nature, as in its present State. O what shall I do, that I may reach this which I so much long for?

Master. My Son, let not the Eye of Nature with the Will of the Wonders depart from that Eye which is introverted into the Divine Liberty, and into the Eternal Light of the holy Majesty: but let it draw to you those Wonders by Union with that heavenly internal Eye, which are externally wrought out and manifested in visible Nature. For while you are in the World, and have an honest Employment, you are certainly by the Order of Providence obliged to labor in it, and to finish the Work given you, according to your best Ability, without repining in the least; seeking out and manifesting for God's Glory, the Wonders of Nature and Are. Since let the Nature be what it will, it is all the Work and Are of God: and let the Art also be what it will, it is still God's Work; and His Art, rather than any Art or Cunning of Man. And all both in Are and Nature serves but abundantly to manifest the wonderful Works of God; that He *for* all, and *in* all may be glorified. Yea, all serves, if you know rightly how to use them, but to recollect you more inwards, and to draw your Spirit into that majestic Light, wherein the original Patterns and Forms of Things visible are to be seen. Keep therefore in the Centre, and stir not out from the Presence of God revealed within your Soul; let the World and the Devil make never so great a Noise and Bustle to draw you out, mind them not; they cannot hurt you. It is permitted to the Eye of your Reason to seek Food, and to your Hands, by their Labor, to get Food for the terrestrial Body: But then this Eye ought not with its Desire to enter into the Food prepared, which would be covetousness; but must in Surrender simply bring it before the Eye of God in your Spirit, and then you must seek to place it close to this very Eye, without letting it go. Mark this Lesson well.

Let the Hands or the Head be at Labor, your Heart ought nevertheless to rest in God. God is a Spirit; dwell in the Spirit, work in the Spirit, pray in the Spirit, and do every

Thing in the Spirit; for remember you also are a Spirit, and thereby created in the Image of God: Therefore see you attract not in your Desire Matter unto you, but as much as possible abstract yourself from all Matter whatever; and so, standing in the Centre, present yourself as a naked Spirit before God, in Simplicity and Purity; and be sure your Spirit draw in nothing but Spirit.

You will yet be greatly enticed to draw Matter, and to gather that which the World calls Substance, thereby to have somewhat visible to trust to: But by no Means consent to the Tempter, nor yield to the Lustings of your Flesh against the Spirit. For in so doing you will infallibly obscure the Divine Light in you; your Spirit will stick in the dark covetous Root, and from the fiery Source of your Soul will it blaze out in Pride and Anger; your Will shall be chained In Earthliness, and shall sink through the Anguish into Darkness and Materiality; and never shall you be able to reach the still Liberty, or to stand before the Majesty of God. Since this is opening a Door for him who reigns in the Corruption of Matter, possibly the Devil may roar at you for this Refusal; because nothing can vex him worse than such a silent Abstraction of the Soul, and Controversion thereof to the Point of Rest from all that is worldly and circumferential: But regard him not; neither admit the least Dust of that Matter into which he may pretend any Claim to. It will be all Darkness to you, as much Matter as is drawn in by the Desire of your Will: It will darken God's Majesty to you; and will close the seeing Eye, by hiding from you the Light of His beloved Countenance. This the Serpent longs to do; but in vain except you permit your Imagination, upon his Suggestion, to receive in the alluring Matter; else he can never get in. Behold then, if you desire to see God's Light in your Soul, and be divinely illuminated and conducted; this is the short Way that you are to take not to let the Eye of your Spirit enter into Matter, or fill itself with any Thing whatever; either in Heaven or Earth; but to let it enter by a naked Faith into the Light of the Majesty; and so receive by pure Love the Light of God, and attract the Divine Power into itself, putting on the Divine Body, and growing up in it to the full Maturity of the Humanity of Christ.

Disciple. As I said before, so I say again, this is very hard. I conceive indeed well enough that my Spirit ought to be free from the Contagion of Matter, and wholly empty, that it may admit into it the Spirit of God. Also, that this Spirit will not enter, but where the Will enters into Nothing, and surrenders itself up in the Nakedness of Faith, and in the Purity of Love, to its Conduct; feeding magically upon the Word of God, and clothing itself thereby with a Divine Substantiality. But, alas, how hard is it for the Will to sink into nothing, to attract nothing, to imagine nothing!

Master. Let it be granted that it is so. Is it not surely worth your while, and all that you can ever do?

Disciple. It is so, I must confess.

Master. But perhaps it may not be as hard as at first it appears to be; make but the Trial, and be in earnest. What is there required of you, but to stand still, and see the Salvation of your God? And could you desire any Thing less? Where is the Hardship in this? You have nothing to care for, nothing to desire in this Life, nothing to imagine or attract: You need only cast your Care upon God, Who cars for you, and leave Him to dispose of you according to His Good Will and Pleasure, even as if you had no Will at all in you. For He knows what is best; and if you can but trust Him, He will most certainly do better for you, than if you were left to your own Choice.

Disciple. This I most firmly believe.

Master. If you believe, then go and do accordingly, All is in the Will, as I have shown you. When the Will imagines after somewhat, then enters it into that somewhat, and this somewhat takes presently the Will into itself, and overclouds it, so as it can have no Light, but must dwell in Darkness, unless it return back out of that somewhat into nothing. But when the Will imagines or lusts after nothing, then it enters into nothing, where it receives the Will of God into itself, and so dwells in Light, and works all its Works in it.

Disciple. I am now satisfied that the main Cause of anyone's spiritual Blindness, is his letting his Will into somewhat, or into that which he has wrought, of whatever Nature it might be, Good or Evil, and his setting his Heart and Affections upon the Work of his own Hands or Brain; and that when the earthly Body perishes, then the Soul must be imprisoned in that very Thing which it shall have received and let in; and if the Light of God be not in it, being deprived of the Light of this World, it cannot but be found in a dark Prison.

Master. This is a very precious Gate of Knowledge; I am glad you take it into such Consideration. The understanding of the whole Scripture is contained in it; and all that has been written from the Beginning of the World to this Day, may be found herein, by him that having entered with his Will into Nothing, has there found All Things, by finding God; from Whom, and to Whom, and in Whom are All Things. By this Means you shall come to hear and see God; and after this earthly Life is ended, to see with the Eye of Eternity all the Wonders of God and of Nature, and more particularly those which shall be wrought by you in the Flesh, or all that the Spirit of God shall have given you to labor out for yourself and your Neighbor, or all that the Eye of Reason enlightened from above, may at any Time have manifested to you. Delay not therefore to enter in by this Gate, which if you see in the Spirit, as some highly favored Souls have seen it, you see in the Supernatural Ground, all that God is, and can do; you see also therewith, as one has said who was taken thereinto, through Heaven, Hell and Earth; and through the Essence of all Essences. Whosoever finds it, has found all that he can desire. Here is the Virtue and Power of the Love of God displayed. Here is the Height and Depth; here is the Breadth and Length thereof manifested, as ever the Capacity of your Soul can contain. By this you shall come into that Ground out of which all Things are originated, and in which they subsist; and in it you shall reign over all God's Works, as a Prince of God.

Disciple. Pray tell me, dear Master where does it dwell in man?

Master. Where Man dwells not: there has it its seat in Man.

Disciple. Where is that in a Man, where Man dwells not in himself?

Master. It is the surrendered Ground of a Soul to which nothing cleaves.

Disciple. Where is the Ground in any Soul, to which there will nothing stick? Or, where is that which abides and dwells not in something?

Master. It is the Centre of Rest and Motion in the surrendered Will of a truly contrite Spirit, which is crucified to the World. This Centre of the Will is impenetrable consequently to the World, the Devil, and

Hell: Nothing in all the World can enter into it, or adhere to it, though never so many Devils should be in the Confederacy against it; because the Will is dead with Christ unto the World, but quickened with Him in the Centre thereof, after His blessed Image. Here it is where Man dwells not; and where no Self abides, or can abide.

Disciple. O where is this naked Ground of the Soul void of all Self? And how shall I come at the hidden Centre where God dwells, and not man? Tell me plainly, loving Sir, where it is, and how it is to be found of me, and entered into?

Master. There where the Soul has slain its own Will, and wills no more any Thing as from itself, but only as God wills, and as His Spirit moves upon the Soul, shall this appear: Where the Love of Self is banished, there dwells the Love of God. For so much of the Soul's own Will as is dead unto itself, even so much room has the Will of God, which is His Love, taken up in that Soul. The Reason whereof is this: Where its own Will did before sit, there is now nothing; and where nothing is, there it is that the Love of God works alone.

Disciple. But how shall I comprehend it?

Master. If you go about to comprehend it, then it will fly away from you; but if you surrender yourself wholly up to it, then it will abide with you, and become the Life of your Life, and be natural to you.

Disciple. And how can this be without dying, or the whole Destruction of my Will?

Master. Upon this entire Surrender and yielding up of your Will, the Love of God in you becomes the Life of your Nature; it does not kill you, but quickens you, who are now dead to yourself in your own Will, according to its proper Life, even the Life of God. And then you live, yet not to your own Will; but you live to His Will; forasmuch as your Will becomes His Will. So then it is no longer your Will, but the Will of God; no longer the Love of yourself, but the Love of God, which moves and operates in you; and then, being thus comprehended in it, you are dead indeed as to yourself, but are alive unto God. So being dead you live, or rather God lives in you by His Spirit; and His Love is made to you Life from the Dead. Never could you with all your seeking, have comprehended it; but it has apprehended you. Much less could you have comprehended it: But now it has comprehended you; and so the Treasure of Treasures is found.

Disciple. How is it that *so few* Souls find it when *so many* would be glad enough to have it?

Master. They all seek it in somewhat, and so they find it not: For where there is somewhat for the Soul to adhere to, there the Soul finds but that somewhat only, and takes up its Rest therein, until it sees that it is to be found in nothing, and goes out of the somewhat into nothing, even into that nothing out of which all Things may be made. The Soul here says, "I have nothing, for I am utterly naked and stripped of every Thing: I can do nothing; for I have no Manner of Power, but am as Water poured out: I am nothing; for all that I am is no more than an Image of Being, and only God is to me I AM; and so sitting down in my own Nothingness, I give Glory to the Eternal Being, and will nothing myself, that so God may will All in me, being unto me my God and All Things." Herein now it is that so very few find this most precious Treasure in the Soul, though everyone would so fain have it; and might also have it, were it not for this something in everyone which obstructs it.

Disciple. But if the Love should proffer itself to a Soul, could not that Soul find it, nor lay hold on it, without going for it into Nothing?

Master. No verily. Men seek and find not, because they seek it not in the naked Ground where it lies; but in something or other where it never will be, neither can be. They seek it in their own Will, and they find it not. They seek it in their Self-Desire, and they meet not with it. They look for it in an Image, or in an Opinion, or in Affection, or a natural Devotion and Fervor, and they lose the Substance by thus hunting after a Shadow. They search for it in something sensible or imaginary, in somewhat which they may have a more peculiar natural Inclination for, and Adhesion to; and so they miss of what they seek, for Want of diving into the Suprasensual and Supernatural Ground where the Treasure is hid. Now, should the Love graciously condescend to Proffer itself to such as these, and even to present itself evidently before the Eye of their Spirit, yet would it find no Place in them at all, neither could it be held by them, or remain with them.

Disciple. Why not, if the Love should be willing and ready to offer itself, and to stay with them?

Master. Because the Imaginariness which is in their own Will has set up itself in the Place thereof: And so this Imaginariness would have the Love in it; but the Love flies away, for it is its Prison. The Love may offer itself; but it cannot abide where the Self-Desire attracts or imagines. That Will which attracts nothing, and to which nothing adheres, is only capable of receiving it; for it dwells only in nothing, as I said, and therefore they find it not.

Disciple. If it dwell only in nothing, what is now the Office of it in nothing?

Master. The Office of the Love here is to penetrate incessantly into something; and if it penetrate into, and find a Place in something which is standing still and at Rest, then its Business is to take Possession thereof. And when it has there taken Possession, then it rejoices therein with its flaming Love-Fire, even as the Sun does in the visible World. And then the Office of it, is without Intermission to enkindle a Fire in this something, which may burn it up; and then, with the Flames thereof exceedingly to enflame itself, and raise the Heat of the Love-Fire by it, even seven Degrees higher.

Disciple. O, loving Master, how shall I understand this?

Master. If it but once kindle a Fire within you, my Son, you shall then certainly feel how it consumes all that which it touches; you shall feel it in the burning up yourself, and swiftly devouring all Egoity, or that which you call *I* and *Me*, as standing in a separate Root, and divided from the Deity, and Fountain of your Being. And when this enkindling is made in you, then the Love does so exceedingly rejoice in your Fire, as you would not for all the World be out of it; yea, would rather suffer yourself to be killed, than to enter into your something again. This Fire now must grow hotter and hotter, till it has perfected its Office with respect to you, and therefore will not give over, till it come to the seventh Degree. Its Flame hence also will be so very great, that it will never leave you, though it should even cost you your temporal Life; but it would go with you in its sweet loving Fire into Death; and if you went also into Hell, it would break Hell in Pieces also for your Sake, Nothing is more certain than this; for it is stronger than Death and Hell.

Disciple. Enough, my dearest Master, I can no longer endure that any Thing should divert me from it. But how shall I find the nearest Way to it?

Master. Where the Way is hardest, there go you; and what the World casts away, that take you up. What the World does, that do you not; but in all Things walk you contrary to the World. So you come the nearest Way to that which you are seeking.

Disciple. If I should in all Things walk contrary to other People, I would be in a very unquiet and sad State; and the World would not fail to account me for a Madman.

Master. I bid you not, Child, to do Harm to anyone, thereby to create to yourself any Misery or Unquietness. This is not what I mean by walking contrary in every Thing to the World. But because the World, as the World, loves only Deceit and Vanity, and walks in false and treacherous Ways; thence, if you have a Mind to act a clean contrary Part to the Ways thereof, without any Exception or Reserve whatsoever, Walk you only in the right Way, which is called the Way of Light, as that of the World is properly the Way of Darkness. For the right Way, even the path of Light is contrary to all the ways of the World.

But whereas you are afraid of creating for yourself Trouble and Inquietude, that indeed, will be according to the Flesh. In the World you must have Trouble, and your Flesh will not fail to be unquiet, and to give you Occasion of continual Repentance. Nevertheless in this very Anxiety of Soul, arising either from the World or the Flesh, the Love does most willingly enkindle itself, and its cheering and conquering Fire is but made to blaze forth with greater Strength for the Destruction of that Evil. And whereas you do also say, that the World will for this esteem you mad; it is true the World will be apt enough to censure you for a Madman in walking contrary to it: And you are not to be surprised if the Children thereof laugh at you, calling you silly Fool. For the way to the Love of God is Folly to the World, but is Wisdom to the Children of God. Hence, whenever the World perceives this Holy Fire of Love in God's Children, it concludes immediately that they are turned Fools, and are besides themselves. But to the Children of God, that which is despised by the World is the Greatest Treasure; yea, so great a Treasure it is, as no Life can express, nor Tongue so much as name what this enflaming, all-conquering Love of God is. It is brighter than the Sun; it is sweeter than any Thing that is called sweet; it is stronger than all Strength; it is more nutrimental than Food; more cheering to the Heart than Wine, and more pleasant than all the Joy and Pleasantness of this World. Whosoever obtains it, is richer than any Monarch on Earth and he who gets it, is nobler than any Emperor can be, and more potent and absolute than all Power and Authority.

OF HEAVEN and HELL

A DIALOGUE BETWEEN A SCHOLAR AND HIS MASTER *SHOWING* w*hither the blessed and the damned Souls go when they depart from their Bodies; and How Heaven and Hell are in Man; Where the Angels and Devils dwell in this World's Time; How far Heaven and Hell are asunder; and What and Whence the Angels and Human Souls are; What the Body of Man is; and Why the Soul is capable of receiving Good and Evil; Of the Destruction of the World; Of Man's Body in and after the Resurrection; Where Heaven and Hell shall be; Of the Last Judgment; and Why the Strife in the Creature must be.*

A DIALOGUE between JUNIUS, a SCHOLAR, and THEOPHORUS, his MASTER

The Scholar asked his Master, saying; Whither goes the Soul when the Body dies?

His master answered him; There is no Necessity for it to go any whither.

What not! *said the inquisitive Junius:* Must not the Soul leave the Body at Death, and go either to Heaven or Hell? It needs no going forth, *replied the venerable*

Theophorus: Only the outward mortal Life with the Body shall separate themselves from the Soul. The Soul has Heaven and Hell within itself before, according as it is written, **"The Kingdom of God comes not with Observation, neither shall they say,** Lo here! or Lo there! For **behold the Kingdom of God is within you."**

And whichever of the two, that is, either Heaven or Hell is manifested in it, in that the Soul stands.

Here ***Junius said to his Master;*** This is hard to understand. Does it not enter into Heaven or Hell, as a Man enters into a House; or as one goes through a Hole or Casement, into an unknown Place; so goes it not into another World?

The Master spoke and said; No. There is verily no such Kind of entering in; forasmuch as Heaven and Hell are everywhere, being universally co-extended.

How is that possible? *said the Scholar.* What, can Heaven and Hell be here present, where we are now sitting? And if one of them might, can you make me believe that both should ever be here together?

Then spoke the Master in this Manner: I have said that Heaven is everywhere present; and it is true. For God is in Heaven; and God is everywhere. I have said also, that Hell must be in like Manner everywhere; and that is also true. For the **wicked One**, who is the Devil, is in Hell; and the whole World, as the Apostle has taught us, lies in the **wicked One**, or the **evil One;** which is as much as to say, not only that the Devil is in the World, but also that the World is in the Devil; and if in the Devil, then in Hell too, because he is there. So Hell therefore is everywhere, as well as Heaven; which is the Thing that was to be proved.

The Scholar, startled hereat, said*,* Pray make me to understand this. ***To whom the Master said****:* Understand then what Heaven is: **It is but the Turning in of the Will into the Love of God**. Wherever you find God manifesting Himself in Love, there you find Heaven, without travelling for it so much as one Foot. And by this understand also what Hell is, and where it is. I say unto you, it is **but the Turning in of the Will into the Wrath of God**. Wherever the Anger of God does more or less manifest itself, there certainly is more or less of Hell, in whatsoever Place it be. So that it is but the Turning in of your Will either into His Love, or into His Anger; and you are accordingly either in Heaven or in Hell. Mark it well. And this now comes to pass in this present Life, whereof St. Paul speaking, says, "**Our Conversation is in Heaven**." And the Lord Christ says also; "**My Sheep HEAR my Voice, and I know them, and they follow me, and I give them the Eternal Life; and none shall pluck them out of my Hand.**" Observe, he says not, **I will give** them - after this Life is ended; but **I give** them, that is, **now** - in the Time of this Life. And what else is this Gift of Christ to His Followers but an Eternity of Life; which for certain, can be nowhere but in Heaven? And also if Christ is in Heaven, and they who follow Him in the Regeneration are in His Hand, then are they where He is, and so cannot be out of Heaven: Yea, moreover none shall be able to pluck them out of Heaven, because it is He who holds them there, and they are in His Hand which nothing can resist. All therefore does consist in the Turning in, or Entering of the Will into Heaven, by HEARING the Voice of Christ, and both **Knowing** Him and **Following** Him. And so on the contrary it is also. Do you understand this?

His Scholar said to him; I think, in part, I do. But how comes this entering of the Will into Heaven to pass?

The Master answered him; This then I will endeavor to satisfy you in; but you must be very attentive to what I shall say unto you. Know then, my Son, that when the Ground of the Will yields itself up to God, then it sinks out of its own Self, and out of and beyond all Ground and

Place that is or can be imagined, into a certain unknown Deep, where God only is manifest, and where He only works and wills. And then it becomes nothing to itself, as to its OWN Working and Willing; and so God works and wills in it. And God dwells in this surrendered Will; by which the soul is sanctified, and so fitted to come into Divine Rest. Now in this Case when the Body breaks, the Soul is thoroughly penetrated all over with the Divine Love, and so thoroughly illuminated with the Divine Light, even as a glowing hot Iron is by the Fire, by which being penetrated throughout, it loses its Darkness and becomes bright and shining. Now this is **the Hand of Christ**, where God's Love thoroughly inhabits the Soul, and is in it a shining Light, and a new glorious Life. And then the Soul is in Heaven, and is a Temple of the Holy Ghost, and is itself the very Heaven of God, wherein He dwells. Lo, this is the entering of the Will into Heaven and how it comes to pass.

Be pleased, Sir, to proceed, *said the Scholar,* and let me know how it fares on the other Side.

The Master said: The godly Soul, you see, is in the **Hand of Christ**, that is in Heaven, as He Himself has told us; and in what Manner this comes to be so, you have also heard. But the ungodly Soul is not willing in this Lifetime to come into the Divine Surrender of its Will, or to enter into the Will of God; but goes on still in its OWN Lust and Desire, in Vanity and Falsehood, and so enters into the Will of the Devil. It receives thereupon into itself nothing but Wickedness; nothing but Lying, Pride, Covetousness, Envy, and Wrath; and into that it gives up its Will and whole Desire. This is the Vanity of the Will; and this same Vanity or vain Shadow must also in like Manner be manifested in the Soul, which has yielded up itself to be its Servant; and must work therein, even as the

Love of God works in the regenerated Will, and penetrates it all over, as Fire does Iron.

And it is not possible for this Soul to come into the **Rest of God**; because God's Anger is manifested in it, and works in it. Now when the Body is parted from this Soul, then begins the Eternal Melancholy and Despair; because it now finds that it is become altogether Vanity, even a Vanity most vexatious to itself, and a distracting Fury, and a Self-tormenting Abomination. Now it perceives itself disappointed of every Thing which it had before fancied, and blind, and naked, and wounded, and hungry, and thirsty; without the least Prospect of being ever relieved, or Obtaining so much as one Drop of Water of Eternal Life. And it feels itself to be a mere Devil to itself, and to be its own Vile Executioner and Tormentor; and is affrighted at its own ugly dark Form, appearing as a most hideous and monstrous Worm, and fain would flee from itself, if it could, but it cannot, being fast bound with the Chains of the Dark Nature, into which it had sunk itself when in the Flesh. And so not having learned nor accustomed itself to sink down into the Divine Grace, and being also strongly possessed with the Idea of God, as an Angry and Jealous God, the poor Soul is both afraid and ashamed to bring its Will into God, by which Deliverance might possibly come to it. The Soul is afraid to do it, as Fearing to be consumed by so doing, under the Apprehension of the Deity as a mere **devouring Fire**. The Soul is also **ashamed** to do it, as being confounded at its own Nakedness and Monstrosity; and therefore would, if it were possible, hide itself from the Majesty of God, and cover its abominable Form from His most holy Eye, though by casting itself still deeper into the Darkness, wherefore then it **will not** enter into God; nay, it cannot enter with its false Will; yea, though it should strive to enter, yet it cannot enter into the Love, because of the Will which has reigned in it. For such a Soul is thereby captivated in the Wrath; yea, is itself but **mere Wrath**, having by its false Desire, which it had awakened in itself, comprehended and shut up itself therewith, and so transformed itself into the Nature and Property thereof.

And since also the Light of God does not shine in it, nor the Love of God incline it, the Soul is moreover a **great Darkness**, and is withal an anxious **Fire-Source**, carrying about a Hell within itself, and not being able to discern the least Glimpse of the Light of God, or to feel the least Spark of His love. Thus it dwells in itself as in Hell, and needs no entering into Hell at all, or being carried thither; for in whatever Place it may be, so long as it is in itself, it is in the Hell. And though it should travel far, and cast itself many hundred thousand Leagues from its present Place, to be out of Hell; yet still would it remain in the Hellish Source and Darkness.

If this be so, how then comes it, *said the Scholar to Theophorus*, that a Heavenly Soul does not in the Time of this Life perfectly perceive the Heavenly Light and Joy; and the Soul which is without God in the World, does not also here feel Hell, as well as hereafter? Why should they not both be perceived and felt as well in this Life as in the next, seeing that both of them are in Man, and one of them (as you have shown) works in every Man?

To whom Theophorus presently returns this Answer: The Kingdom of Heaven is in the Saints operative and manifestative of itself by **Faith**. They who carry God within them, and live by His Spirit, find the **Kingdom of God** in their **Faith**; and they feel the Love of God in their **Faith**, by which the Will has given up itself into God, and is made Godlike. In a Word, all is transacted within them **by Faith**, which is to them the Evidence of the Eternal Invisibles, and a great Manifestation in their Spirit of this Divine Kingdom, which is within them. But their natural Life is nevertheless encompassed with Flesh and Blood; and this Standing in a Contrariety thereto, and being placed through the Fall in the Principle of God's Anger, and surrounded about with the World, which by no means can be reconciled to Faith, these faithful Souls cannot but be very much exposed to Attacks from this World, wherein they are Sojourners; neither can they be insensible of their being thus compassed about with Flesh and Blood, and with this World's vain Lust, which ceases not continually to penetrate the outward mortal Life, and to tempt them in manifold Ways, even as it did Christ. Whence the World on one side, and Devil on the other, not without the Curse of God's Anger in Flesh and Blood, do thoroughly penetrate and sift the Life; whereby it comes to pass that the Soul is often in Anxiety when these three are all set upon it together, and when Hell thus assaults the Life, and would manifest itself in the Soul. But the Soul hereupon sinks down into the Hope of the Grace of God, and stands like a beautiful Rose in the Midst of Thorns, until the Kingdom of this World shall fall from it in the Death of the Body; And then the Soul first becomes truly manifest in the Love of God, and in His Kingdom, which is the Kingdom of Love; having henceforth nothing more to hinder it. But during this Life she must walk with Christ in this World; and then Christ delivers her out of her own Hell, by penetrating her with His Love throughout, and standing by her in Hell, and even changing her Hell into Heaven.

But in that you ask, *why do not the Souls which are without God feel Hell in this World*? I answer; They bear it about with them in their wicked Consciences, but they know it not; because the World has put out their Eyes, and its deadly Cup has cast them likewise into a Sleep, a most fatal Sleep. Notwithstanding which it must be owned that the Wicked do frequently feel Hell within them during the Time of this mortal Life, though they may not apprehend that it is Hell, because of the earthly Vanity which cleaves unto them from without, and the sensible Pleasures and Amusements wherewith they are intoxicated. And moreover it is to be noted, that the outward Life in every such one has yet the Light of the outward Nature, which rules in that Life; and so the Pain of Hell cannot, so long as that has Rule, be revealed. But when the Body dies or breaks away, so as the Soul cannot any longer enjoy such temporal Pleasure and Delight, nor the Light of this outward World, which is wholly thereupon extinguished as to it; then the Soul stands in an eternal Hunger and Thirst after such Vanities as it was here in Love withal, but yet can reach nothing but that false Will, which it had impressed in itself while in the Body; and wherein it had abounded to its great Loss. And now whereas it had too much of its Will in this Life, and yet was not contented therewith, it has after this Separation by Death, as little of it; which creates in it an everlasting Thirst after that which it can henceforth never more obtain, and causes it to be in a perpetual anxious Lust after Vanity, according to its former Impression, and in a continual Rage of Hunger after those Sorts of Wickedness and Lewdness into which it was immersed, while being in the Flesh. Fain would it do more Evil still, but that it has not either wherein or wherewith to effect the Same, left to it; and therefore it does perform this only **in itself**. All is now internally transacted, as if it were outward; and so the Ungodly Soul is tormented by those Furies which are in his own Mind, and begotten upon himself by himself. For he is verily become his own Devil and Tormentor; and that by which he sinned here, when the Shadow of this World is passed away, abides still with him in the Impression, and is made his Prison and his Hell. But this hellish Hunger and Thirst cannot be fully manifested in the Soul, till the Body which ministered to the Soul what it lusted after, and with which the Soul was so bewitched, as to dote thereupon, and pursue all its Cravings, be stripped off from it.

I perceive then, *said Junius to his Master,* that the Soul having played the Wanton with the Body in all Voluptuousness, and having served the Lusts thereof during this Life, retains still the very same Inclinations and Affections which it had before; so that when it has no more Opportunity nor Capacity to satisfy them; and when it finds it cannot, then Hell will open in that Soul, which before had been shut up, by Means of the outward Life in the Body, and of the Light of this World. Do I rightly understand?

Theophorus said, It is very rightly understood by you. Go on.

On the other hand, *the Scholar went on,* I clearly perceive by what I have heard, that Heaven cannot but be in a loving Soul, which is possessed of God, and has subdued thereby the Body to the Obedience of the Spirit in all Things, and perfectly immersed itself into the Will and Love of God. And when the Body dies, and this Soul is hence redeemed from the Earth, it is now evident to me, that the Life of God which was hidden in it, will display Itself gloriously, and Heaven will consequently be then manifested. But notwithstanding, if there be not also a local Heaven besides, and a local Hell, I am still at a loss where to place no small Part of the Creation, if not the greatest. For where must all the intellectual Inhabitants abide?

In their own Principle, *answered the Master*, whether it be of Light or of Darkness. For every created intellectual Being remains in its Deeds and Essences, in its Wonders and Properties, in its Life and Image; and therein it beholds and feels God, as Who is everywhere, whether it be in the Love, or in the Wrath.

If it be in the Love of God, then beholds it God accordingly, and feels Him as He is Love. But if it has captivated itself in the Wrath of God, then it cannot behold God otherwise than in the wrathful Nature, nor perceive Him otherwise than as an incensed and vindictive Spirit. All Places are alike to it, if it be in God's Love; and if it be not there, every Place is Hell alike. What Place can bound a Thought? Or what needs any understanding Spirit to be kept here or there, in order to its Happiness or Misery? Verily, Wherever it is, it is in the **abyssal** World, where there is neither End nor Limit. And whither, I pray, should it go? Since though it should go a thousand Miles off, or a thousand Times ten thousand Miles, and this ten thousand Times over, beyond the Bounds of the Universe, and into the imaginary Spaces above the Stars, yet it were then still in the very same Point from whence it went out. For God is **the Place** of **Spirit**; if it may be lawful to attribute to Him such a Name, to which the Body has a Relation: And in God there is no Limit; both near and far off is here all one; and be it in His Love, or be it in His Anger, the **abyssal Will** of the Spirit is altogether unconfined. It is swift as Thought, passing through all Things; it is magical, and nothing corporeal or from without can let or obstruct it; it dwells in its Wonders, and they are its House.

Thus it is with every Intellectual, whether of the Order of Angels, or of human Souls; and you need not fear but there will be Room enough for them all, be they ever so many; and such also as shall best suit them, even according to their Election and Determination; and which may thence very well be called his **own Place**.

At which, *said the Scholar;* I remember, indeed, that it is written concerning the great Traitor, that he went after Death to his **own Place**.

The Master here said: The same is true of every Soul, when it departs this mortal Life: And it is true in like Manner of every Angel, or Spirit whatsoever; which is necessarily determined by its own Choice. As God is everywhere, so also the Angels are everywhere; but each one in its own Principle, and in its own Property, or (if you had rather) in **its own Place**. The same Essence of God, which is a Place of Spirits, is confessed to be everywhere; but the Appropriation, or Participation thereof is different to everyone, according as each has attracted magically in the Earnestness of the Will. The same Divine Essence which is with the Angels of God above, is with us also below: And the same Divine Nature which is with us, is likewise with them; but after different Manners and in different Degrees, communicated and participated.

And what I have said here of the **Divine**, is no less to be considered by you in the Participation of the Diabolical Essence and Nature, which is the **Power of Darkness**, as to the manifold Modes, Degrees, and Appropriations thereof in the false Will. In this World there is Strife between them: but when this World has reached in any one the Limit, then the Principle catches that which is its own: and so the Soul receives Companions accordingly, that is, either Angels or Devils.

To whom the Scholar said again: Heaven and Hell then being in us at Strife in the Time of this Life, and God Himself being also thus near unto us, where can Angels and Devils dwell?

And the Master answered him thus: Where you do not dwell as to your **Selfhood**, and to your **OWN Will**, there the holy Angels dwell with you, and everywhere all over round about you. Remember this well. On the contrary, where you dwell as to yourself, in Self-Seeking, and Self-Will, there to be sure the Devils will be with you, and will take up their abode with you, and dwell all over you, and round about you everywhere. Which may God in his Mercy prevent!

I understand not this, *said the Scholar,* so perfectly well as I could wish. Be pleased to make it a little more clear to me.

The Master then spoke: Mark well what I am going to say. Where the Will of God in any Thing wills, there is God manifested; and in this very manifestation of God, the Angels do dwell. But where God in any Creature wills not with the Will of that Creature, there God is not manifested to it, neither can He be; but dwells in Himself, without the Cooperation and Subjection of the Creature to Him in Humility. There God is an unmanifest God to the Creature. So the Angels dwell not with such a one; for wherever they dwell, there is the Glory of God; and they make His Glory. What then dwells in such a Creature as this? God dwells not therein; the Angels dwell not therein; God wills not therein, the Angels also will not therein. The case is evidently this, in that Soul or Creature its OWN Will is without God's Will, and there the Devil dwells; and with him all whatever is without God, and without Christ. This is the Truth; lay it to Heart.

The Scholar: It is possible I may ask several impertinent Questions; but I beseech you, good Sir, to have Patience with me, and to pity my Ignorance, if I ask what may appear to you perhaps ridiculous, or may not seem fit for me to expect an Answer to. For I have several Questions still to propound to you; but I am ashamed of my own Thoughts in this Matter.

The Master: Be plain with me, and propose whatever is upon your Mind; yea, be not ashamed even to appear ridiculous, so that by Querying you may but become wiser.

The Scholar thanked his Master for this Liberty, and said: How far then are Heaven and Hell asunder?

To whom he answered thus: As far as Day and Night; or as far as Something and Nothing. They are in one another, and yet they are at the greatest Distance one from the other. Nay, the one of them is as nothing to the other; and yet they cause Joy and Grief to one another. Heaven is throughout the whole World, and It is also without the World over all, even everywhere that is, or that can be but so much as imagined. It fills all; It is within all; It is without all; It encompasses all; without Division, without Place; working by a Divine Manifestation, and flowing forth universally, but not going in the least out of Itself. For It works only in Itself, and is revealed, being ONE, and undivided in ALL. It appears only through the Manifestation of God; and never but in Itself only: And in that Being which comes into It, or in that wherein It is manifested, there also it is that God is manifested. Because Heaven is nothing else but a Manifestation or

Revelation of the Eternal ONE, wherein ALL the Working and Willing is in quiet LOVE.

So in like Manner Hell also is through the whole World, and dwells and works but in itself, and in that wherein the Foundation of Hell is manifested, namely, in Self-hood, and in the False Will. The visible World has both in it; and there is no Place but what Heaven and Hell may be found or revealed in it. Now Man as to his temporal Life, is only of the visible World; and therefore during the Time of this Life, he sees not the spiritual World. For the outward World with its Substance, is a Cover to the spiritual World, even as the Body is to the Soul. But when the outward Man dies, then the spiritual World, as to the Soul, which has now its Covering taken away, is manifested either in the Eternal Light with the holy Angels, or in the Eternal Darkness, with the Devils.

The Scholar further queried: What is an Angel, or a human Soul that they can be thus manifested either in God's Love or Anger, either in Light or Darkness?

To whom Theophorus answered: They come from one and the Self-same Original: They are little Branches of the Divine Wisdom, of the Divine Will, sprung from the Divine Word, and made Objects of the Divine Love. They are out of the Ground of Eternity, whence Light and Darkness do spring: Darkness, which consists in the receiving of Self-Desire: and Light, which consists in Willing the same Thing with God. For in the conformity of the Will with God's Will, is Heaven; and Wherever there is this Willing with God, there the Love of God is undoubtedly in the Working, and His Light will not fail to manifest Itself. But in the Self-Attraction of the Soul's Desire, or in the Reception of Self into the Willing of any Spirit, Angelical or Human, the Will of God works difficultly, and is to that Soul or Spirit nothing but Darkness; out of which, notwithstanding, the Light may be manifested. And this Darkness is the Hell of that Spirit wherein it is. For **Heaven** and **Hell** are nothing else but a **Manifestation of the Divine Will either in Light or Darkness, according to the Properties of the Spiritual World**.

What the Body of Man is; and why the Soul is capable of receiving Good and Evil.

Scholar. WHAT then is the Body of Man?

Master. It is the visible World; an Image and Quintessence, or Compound of all that the World is; and the visible World is a Manifestation of the inward spiritual World, come out of the eternal Light, and out of the eternal Darkness, out of the spiritual Compaction or Connection; and it is also an Image or Figure of Eternity, whereby Eternity has made itself visible; where Self-Will and SURRENDERED Will, viz. Evil and Good, work one with the other. Such a Substance is the outward Man. For God created Man of the outward World, and breathed into him the inward spiritual World for a Soul and intelligent Life; and therefore in the Things of the outward World, Man can receive and work Evil and Good.

Of the Destruction of the World; of Man's Body, in and after the Resurrection; where Heaven and Hell shall be; of the Last Judgment; and wherefore the Strife in the Creature must be.

Scholar. WHAT shall be after this World, when all Things perish and come to an End?

Master. The material Substance only ceases; **viz.** the four Elements, the Sun, Moon, and Stars. And then the inward

World will be wholly visible and manifest. But whatsoever has been wrought by the Will or Spirit of a Man in this World's Time, whether evil or good shall not cease. I say, every such Work shall there separate itself in a spiritual Manner, either into the Eternal Light, or into the Eternal Darkness. For that which is born from each Man's Will shall penetrates and passes again into that which is like itself. And there the Darkness is called Hell, and is an **eternal forgetting of all Good**; and the Light is called the Kingdom of God, and is an eternal Joy in and to the Saints, who continually glorify and praise God, for having delivered them from the Torment of Evil. The Last Judgment is but a Kindling of the Fire both of God's Love and Anger, in which the Matter of every Substance perishes, and each Fire shall attract into itself its own, that is, the Substance that is like itself: Thus God's Fire of Love will draw into It whatsoever is born in the Love of God, or Love-Principle, in which also It shall burn after the Manner of Love, and yield Itself into that Substance. But the Torment will draw into itself what is wrought in the Anger of God in Darkness, and consume the false Substance; and then there will remain only the painful aching Will in its own proper Nature, Image and Figure.

Scholar. With what Matter and Form shall the human Body rise?

Master. It is sown a natural gross and elementary Body, which in this Lifetime is like the outward Elements; yet in this gross Body there is a subtle Power and Virtue. As in the Earth also there is a subtle good Virtue, which is like the Sun, and is one and the same with the Sun; which also in the Beginning of Time did spring and proceed out of the Divine Power and Virtue, from whence all the good Virtue of the Body is likewise derived. This good Virtue of the mortal Body shall come again and live forever in a

Kind of transparent crystalline material Property, in spiritual Flesh and Blood; as shall return also the good Virtue of the Earth, for the Earth likewise shall become crystalline, and the Divine Light shine in every Thing that has a Being, Essence or Substance. And as the gross Earth shall perish and never return, so also the gross Flesh of Man shall perish and not live forever. But all Things must appear before the Judgment, and in the Judgment be separated by the Fire; yea, both the Earth, and also the Ashes of the human Body. For when God shall once move the spiritual World, every Spirit shall attract its spiritual Substance to itself. A good Spirit and Soul shall draw to itself its good Substance, and an evil one its evil Substance. But we must here understand by Substance, such a material Power and Virtue, the Essence of which is mere Virtue, like a material Tincture (such a Thing as has all Figures, Colors, and Virtues in it, and is at the same Time transparent), the Grossness whereof shall have perished in all Things.

Scholar. Shall we not rise again with our visible Bodies, and live in them forever?

Master. When the visible World perishes, then all that has come out of it, and has been external, shall perish with it. There shall remain of the World only the heavenly crystalline Nature and Form, and of Man also only the spiritual Earth; for Man shall be then wholly like the spiritual World, which as yet is hidden.

Scholar. Shall there be Husband and Wife, or Children or Kindred, in the heavenly Life, or shall one associate with another, as they do in this Life?

Master. Why are you so fleshly-minded? There will be neither Husband nor Wife, but all will be like the Angels of God, Viz. Masculine Virgins. There will be neither Son nor Daughter, Brother nor Sister, but all of one Stock and Kindred. For all are but One in Christ, as a Tree and its Branches are one, though distinct as Creatures; but God is All in All. Indeed, there will be spiritual Knowledge of what everyone has been, and done, but no Possessing or Enjoying, or Desire of Possessing earthly Things, or Enjoying fleshly Relations any more.

Scholar. Shall they all have that Eternal Joy and Glorification alike?

Master. The Scripture says, "**Such as the People is, such is their God.**"

And in another Place, "**With the holy you are holy, and with the perverse you are perverse.**"

And St. Paul says, "**In the Resurrection one shall differ from another in Glory, as do the Sun, Moon, and Stars.**"

Therefore know, that the Blessed shall indeed all enjoy the Divine Working in and upon them; but their Virtue, and Illumination or Glory, shall be very different, according as they have been endued in this Life with different Measures and Degrees of Power and Virtue in their painful Working. For the painful Working of the Creature in this Lifetime is the opening and begetting of Divine Power, by which that Power is made movable and operative. Now those who have wrought with Christ in this Lifetime, and not in the Lust of the Flesh, shall have great Power and transcendent Glorification in and upon them. But others, who have only expected, and relied upon, an imputed Satisfaction, and in the meanwhile have served their Belly-God, and yet at last have turned, and obtained Grace; those, I say, shall not attain to so high a Degree of Power and Illumination. So that there will be as great a Difference of Degrees between them, as is between the Sun, Moon and Stars; or between the Flowers of the Field in their Varieties of Beauty, Power, and Virtue.

Scholar. How shall the World be judged, and by Whom?

Master. **Jesus Christ**, that "**Word of God which became Man**," shall by the Power of His Divine Stirring or Motion separate from Himself all that belongs not to Him, and shall wholly manifest His Kingdom in the Place or Space where this World now is; for the separating Motion works all over the Universe, through all at once.

Scholar. Whither shall the Devils and all the Damned be thrown, when the Place of this World is become the Kingdom of Christ, and as Such shall be glorified? Shall they be cast out of the Place of this World? Or shall Christ have, and manifest His Dominion, out of the Sphere or Place of this World?

Master. Hell shall remain in the Place or Sphere of this World everywhere, but hidden to the Kingdom of Heaven, as the Night is hidden in and to the Day. "**The Light shall shine forever in the Darkness, but the Darkness can never comprehend, or reach it**." And the Light is the Kingdom of Christ; but the Darkness is Hell, wherein the Devils and the Wicked dwell; and thus they shall be suppressed by the Kingdom of Christ, and made his Footstool, viz. a Reproach.

Scholar. How shall all People and Nations be brought to Judgment?

Master. The Eternal Word of God, out of which every spiritual creaturely Life has proceeded, will move Itself at that Hour, according to Love and Anger, in every Life which is come out of the Eternity, and will draw every Creature before the Judgment of Christ, to be sentenced by this Motion of the World. The Life will then be manifested in all its Works, and every Soul shall see and feel its Judgment and Sentence in itself. For the Judgment is indeed immediately manifested in and to every Soul at the Departure of the Body; and the last Judgment is but a Return of the spiritual Body, and a Separation of the World, when the Evil shall be separated from the Good, in the substance of the World and of the human Body, and every Thing enters into its eternal Receptacle. And thus it is a Manifestation of the Mystery of God in every Substance and Life.

Scholar. How will the Sentence be pronounced?

Master. Here consider the Words of Christ:

"He will say to those on His Right hand, Come, you blessed of My Father, inherit the Kingdom prepared for you from the Foundation of the World. For I was hungry, and you gave Me Meat; I was thirsty, and you gave Me Drink; I was a Stranger, and you took Me in; naked, and you clothed Me. I was sick, and you visited Me, in Prison, and you came unto Me".

Then shall they answer Him, saying, **"Lord, when saw we You hungry, thirsty, a Stranger, naked, sick, or in Prison, and ministered thus unto You?"**

And shall the King answer and say unto them; **"Inasmuch as you have done it unto one of the least of these my Brethren, you have done it unto Me."**

And unto the Wicked on His Left hand He will say, **"Depart from Me, you Cursed, into everlasting Fire, prepared for the Devil and his Angels. For I was**

hungry, thirsty, a Stranger, naked, sick, and in Prison, and you ministered not unto Me."

And they shall also answer Him and say, " **When did we see You thus, and ministered not unto You?**"

And He will answer them, "**Verily I say unto you, inasmuch as you have not done it unto one of the least of these, you did it not to Me." And these shall depart into everlasting Punishment, but the Righteous into Life Eternal**.

Scholar. Loving Master, pray tell me why Christ says, "**What you have done to the least of these, you have done to Me; and what you have not done to them, neither have you done it to Me.**" And how does a Man in his Working, do it to **Christ Himself**?

Master. Christ dwells really and essentially in the Faith of those that wholly yield up themselves to Him, and He gives them His Flesh for Food, and His Blood for Drink; and thus He possesses the Ground of their Faith, according to the interior or inward Man. And a True Christian is called a Branch of the Vine Christ, and a Christian, because Christ dwells spiritually in him; therefore whatsoever Good any shall do to such a Christian in his bodily Necessities, it is done to Christ Himself, Who dwells in him. For such a Christian is not his own, but is wholly surrendered to Christ, and become His peculiar Possession, and consequently the good Deed is done to Christ **Himself**. Therefore also, whosoever shall withhold their Help from such a needy Christian, and forbear to serve him in his Necessity, they thrust Christ away from themselves, and despise Him in His Members. When a poor Person that belongs thus to Christ, asks any Thing of you, and you deny it to him in his Necessity, you deny it to Christ Himself. And whatsoever hurt any shall do to such a Christian, they do it to Christ Himself. When any mock, scorn, revile, reject, or thrust away such a one, they do all that to Christ; but he that receives him, gives him Meat and Drink, or Apparel, and assists him in his necessities, does it likewise to Christ, and to a Fellow-Member of his own Body. Nay he even does it to himself, if he be a True Christian; for we are all One in Christ, as a Tree and its Branches are.

Scholar. How then will those subsist in the Day of that fierce Judgment, who afflict and vex the poor and distressed, and deprive them of their very Sweat; necessitating and constraining them by Force to submit to their Wills, and trampling upon them as their Footstools, only that they themselves may live in Pomp and Power, and spend the Fruits of this poor People's Sweat and Labor in Voluptuousness, Pride, and Vanity?

Master. Christ suffers in the Persecution of His Members. Therefore all the Wrong that such hard Exactors do to the poor Wretches under their Control, is done to Christ Himself; and falls under His severe Sentence and Judgment! And besides that, they help the Devil to augment his Kingdom; for by such Oppression of the Poor they draw them off from Christ, and make them seek unlawful Ways to fill their Bellies. Nay, they work for, and with the Devil himself, doing the very same Thing which he does; who, without Intermission, opposes the Kingdom of Christ, which consists only in Love. All these Oppressors, if they do not turn with their whole Hearts to Christ, and minister to, or serve Him, must go into Hell-Fire, which is fed and kept alive by nothing else but such mere Self, as that which they have exercised over the Poor here.

Scholar. But how will it fare with those, and how will they be able to stand that severe Trial, who in this Time do so fiercely contend about the Kingdom of Christ, and slander, revile, and persecute one another for their Religion, as they do?

Master. All such have not yet known Christ; and they are but as a Type or Figure of Heaven and Hell, striving with each other for the Victory. All rising, swelling Pride, which contends about Opinions, is an Image of Self. And whosoever has not Faith and Humility, nor lives in the Spirit of Christ, which is Love, is only armed with the Anger of God, and helps forward the Victory of the imaginary Self, that is, the Kingdom of Darkness, and the Anger of God. For at the Day of Judgment all Self shall be given to the Darkness, as shall also all the unprofitable Contentions of Men; in which they seek not after Love, but merely after their imaginary Self, that they may exalt themselves by exalting and establishing their OWN Opinions; even stirring up Princes to Wars for the Sake of the same, and by that Means occasioning the Desolation of whole Countries of People. All such Things belong to the Judgment, which will separate the False from the True; and then all Images or Opinions shall cease, and all the Children of God shall dwell forever in the Love of Christ, and That in them. All whosoever in this Time of Strife, namely, from the Fall to the Resurrection, are not zealous in the Spirit of Christ, and desirous to promote Peace and Love, but seek and strive for themselves only, are of the Devil, and belong to the Pit of Darkness, and must consequently be separated from Christ. For in Heaven all serve God their Creator in Humble Love.

Scholar. Wherefore then does God suffer such Strife and Contention to be in this Time?

Master. The Life itself stands in Strife, that it may be made manifest, sensible, and palpable, and that the Wisdom may be made separable and known.

The Strife also constitutes the eternal Joy of the Victory. For there will arise great Praise and Thanksgiving in the Saints from the experimental Sense and Knowledge that Christ in them has overcome Darkness, and all the Self of Nature, and that they are at length totally delivered from the Strife; at which they shall rejoice eternally, when they shall know how the Wicked are recompensed. And therefore God suffers all Souls to stand in the Free-Will, that the eternal Dominion both of Love and Anger, of Light and Darkness, may be made manifest and known; and that every Life might cause and find its own Sentence in itself. For that which is now a Strife and Pain to the Saints in their wretched Warfare here, shall in the End be turned into great Joy to them; and that which has been a Joy and Pleasure to ungodly Persons in this World, shall afterwards be turned into eternal Torment and Shame to them. Therefore the Joy of the Saints must arise to them out of Death, as the Light arises out of a Candle by the Destruction and Consumption of it in its Fire; that so the Life may be freed from the Painfulness of Nature, and possess another World.

And as the Light has quite another Property than the Fire has, for It gives and yields Itself forth; whereas the Fire draws in and consumes itself; so the holy Life of Meekness springs forth through the Death of Self-Will, and then God's Will of Love only rules, and does ALL in ALL. For thus the Eternal ONE has attained Feeling and Separability, and brought Itself forth again with the Feeling, through Death in great Joyfulness; that there might be an Eternal Delight in the Infinite Unity, and an Eternal Cause of Joy; and therefore that which was before

Painfulness, must now be the Ground and cause of this Motion or stirring to the Manifestation of all Things. And herein lies the Mystery of the hidden Wisdom of God.

Every one that asks receives, every one that seeks finds; and to everyone that knocks it shall be opened. The Grace of our Lord Jesus Christ, and the Love of God, and the Communion of the Holy Ghost, be with us all. **Amen.**

Hebrews 12:22-24 *But you are come to Mount Zion, and to the City of the Living God, the heavenly Jerusalem, and to an innumerable company of angels, to the general assembly and church of the firstborn, whose names are written in heaven, and to God the Judge of all, and to the spirits of just men made perfect, and to Jesus the Mediator of the new covenant, and to the blood of sprinkling, that speaks better things than the blood of Abel. Amen.*

Praise, Glory, and Thanksgiving, Wisdom, Honor and Power unto Him that sits on the throne, to our God, and to the Lamb forever and ever.

THE WAY FROM DARKNESS TO LIGHT
A DISCOURSE BETWEEN A SOUL HUNGRY AND THIRSTY AFTER THE FOUNTAIN OF LIFE, THE SWEET LOVE OF JESUS CHRIST, AND A SOUL ENLIGHTENED SHOWING: *Which Way one Soul should seek after and comfort another, and bring it by Means of its Knowledge into the Paths of Christ's Pilgrimage, and faithfully warn it of the thorny Way of the World, which leads the fallen Soul that naturally walks therein, into the Abyss or Pit of Hell.*

There was a poor Soul that had wandered out of Paradise and come into the Kingdom of this World; where the Devil met with it, and said to it, "Whither do you go, you Soul that are half blind?"

The Soul said: I would see and speculate into the Creatures of the World, which the Creator has made.

The Devil said: How will you see and speculate into them, when you cannot know their Essence and Property? You will look upon their Outside only, as upon a graven Image, and cannot know them thoroughly.

The Soul said: How may I come to know their Essence and Property?

The Devil said: Your Eyes would be opened to see them thoroughly, if you did but eat of that from whence the Creatures themselves are come to be good and evil. You would then be as God Himself is, and know what the Creature is.

The Soul said: I am now a noble and holy Creature; but if I should do so, the Creator has said, that I should die.

The Devil said: No, you should not die at all; but your eyes would be opened, and you should be as God Himself is, and be Master of Good and Evil. Also, you should be mighty, powerful, and very great, as I am; all the Subtlety that is in the Creatures would be made known to you.

The Soul said: If I had the Knowledge of Nature and of the Creatures, I would then rule the whole World as I pleased.

The Devil said: The whole Ground of that Knowledge lies in you. Do but turn your Will and Desire from God or Goodness into Nature and the Creatures, and then there will arise in you a Lust to taste; and so you may eat of the Tree of Knowledge of Good and Evil, and by that means come to know all Things.

The Soul said: Well then, I will eat of the Tree of Knowledge of Good and Evil, that I may rule all Things by my own Power; and be of myself a Lord on Earth, and do what I will, as God Himself does.

The Devil said: I am the Prince of this World; and if you would rule on Earth, you must turn your Lust towards my Image, or desire to be like me, that you may get the Cunning, Wit, Reason, and Subtlety, that my Image has. Thus did the Devil present to the Soul the Vulcan in the Mercury (the Power that is in the fiery Root of the Creature), that is the fiery Wheel of Essence or Substance, in the Form of a Serpent.

Upon which, **The Soul said:** Behold, this is the Power, which can do all Things. What must I do to get it?

The Devil said: You yourself are also such a fiery Mercury. If you do break your Will off from God, and bring it into this Power and Skill, then your hidden

Ground will be manifested in you, and you may work in the same Manner. But you must eat of that Fruit, wherein each of the four Elements in itself rules over the other, and is in Strife; the Heat striving against the Cold, and the Cold against the Heat; and so all the Properties of Nature work feelingly. And then you will instantly be as the fiery Wheel is, and so bring all Things into your own Power, and possess them as your own.

The Soul did so, and what happened thereupon. Now when the Soul broke its Will thus off from God, and brought it into the Mercury, or the fiery Will (which is the Root of Life and Power), there presently arose in it a Lust to eat of the Tree of Knowledge of Good and Evil; and the Soul did eat thereof. Which as soon as it had done so, Vulcan (or the artificer in the fire) instantly kindled the fiery Wheel of its substance, and thereupon all the Properties of Nature awoke in the Soul and each began to exercise its own Lust and Desire.

First arose the Lust of Pride; a Desire to be great, mighty and powerful; to bring all Things under Subjection to it, and so to be Lord itself without Control; despising all Humility and Equality, as esteeming itself the only prudent, witty and cunning One, and accounting every Thing Folly that is not according to its own Humor and Liking.

Secondly arose the Lust of Covetousness; a Desire of Getting, which would draw all Things to itself, into its own Possession. For when the Lust of Pride had turned away the Will from God, then the Life of the Soul would not trust God any further, but would now begin to take Care for itself; and therefore brought its Desire into the Creatures, viz. into the Earth, Metals, Trees, and other Creatures. Thus the kindled fiery Life became hungry and covetous, when it had broken itself off from the Unity, Love and Meekness of God, and attracted to itself the four Elements and their Essence, and brought itself into the Condition of the Beasts; and so the Life became dark, empty and wrathful; and the heavenly Virtues and Colors went out, like a Candle extinguished.

Thirdly, there awoke in this fiery Life the stinging thorny Lust of Envy; a hellish Poison, a Property which all Devils have, and a Torment which makes the Life a mere Enmity to God, and to all Creatures. Which Envy raged furiously in the Desire of Covetousness, as a venomous Sting does in the Body. Envy cannot endure, but hates and would hurt or destroy that which Covetousness cannot draw to itself, by which hellish Passion the noble Love of the Soul is smothered.

Fourthly, there awoke in this fiery Life a Torment like Fire, viz. Anger; which would murder and remove out of the Way all who would not be subject to Pride. Thus the Ground and Foundation of Hell, which is called the Anger of God, was wholly manifested in this Soul. Whereby it lost the fair Paradise of God and the Kingdom of Heaven, and became such a Worm as the fiery Serpent was, which the Devil had presented to it in his own Image and Likeness. And so the Soul began to rule on Earth in a bestial Manner, and did all Things according to the Will of the Devil; living in mere Pride, Covetousness, Envy, and Anger, having no longer any true Love towards God. But there arose in the Stead thereof an evil bestial Love of filthy Lechery, Wantonness, and Vanity, and there was no Purity left in the Heart; for the Soul had forsaken Paradise, and taken the Earth into its Possession. Its Mind was wholly bent upon cunning Knowledge, Subtlety, and getting together a Multitude of earthly Things. No Righteousness nor Virtue remained in it at all; but whatsoever Evil and Wrong it committed, it covered all cunningly and subtly under the Cloak of its Power and Authority by Law, and called it by the Name of Right and Justice, and accounted it good.

THE DEVIL CAME TO THE SOUL.

Upon this the Devil drew near to the Soul, and brought it on from one Vice to another; for he had taken it captive in his Essence, and set Joy and Pleasure before it therein, saying thus to it: Behold, now you are powerful, mighty and noble; endeavor to be greater, richer, and more powerful still. Display your Knowledge, Wit, and Subtlety, that every one may fear you, and stand in Awe of you, and that you may be respected, and get a great Name in the World.

The Soul did so. The Soul did as the Devil counseled it, and yet knew not that its Counselor was the Devil; but thought it was guided by its own Knowledge, Wit, and Understanding, and that it was doing very well and right all the While.

Jesus Christ met with the Soul: The Soul going on in this Course of Life, our dear and loving Lord Jesus Christ, Who was come into this World with the Love and Wrath of God, to destroy the Works of the Devil, and to execute Judgment upon all ungodly Deeds, on a Time met with it, and spoke by a strong Power, viz. by His Passion and Death, into it and destroyed the Works of the Devil in it, and discovered to it the Way to His Grace, and shone upon it with His Mercy, calling it to return and repent; and promising that He would then deliver it from that monstrous deformed Shape or Image which it had gotten, and bring it into Paradise again.

How Christ wrought in the Soul: Now when the Spark of the Love of God, or the Divine Light, was accordingly manifested in the Soul, it presently saw itself with its Will and Works to be in Hell, in the Wrath of God, and found that it as a misshapen ugly Monster in the Divine Presence and the Kingdom of Heaven; at which it was so afraid, that it fell into the greatest Anguish possible, for the Judgment of God was manifested in it.

What Christ said: Upon this the Lord Christ spoke into it with the Voice of His Grace, and said, "Repent and forsake Vanity, and you shall attain My Grace."

What the Soul said: Then the Soul in its ugly misshapen Image, with the defiled Coat of Vanity, went before God, and entreated for Grace and the Pardon of its Sins, and came to be strongly persuaded in itself, that the Satisfaction and Atonement of our Lord Jesus Christ did belong to it. But the evil Properties of the Serpent, formed in the astral Spirit or Reason of the outward Man, would not suffer the Will of the Soul to come before God, but brought their Lusts and Inclinations thereinto. For those evil Properties would not die to their own Lusts, nor leave the World, for they were come out of the World, and therefore they feared the Reproach of it, in case they should have to forsake their worldly Honor and Glory.

But the poor Soul turned its Countenance towards God, and desired Grace from Him, even that He should bestow His Love upon it.

The Devil came to it again: But when the Devil saw that the Soul thus prayed to God, and would enter into Repentance, he drew near to it, and thrust the Inclinations of the earthly Properties into its Prayers, and disturbed its good Thoughts and Desires which pressed forward towards God, and drew its thoughts back again to earthly Things that they might have no Access to Him.

The Soul sighed: The central Will of the Soul indeed sighed after God, but the Thoughts arising in the Mind, that it should penetrate into Him, were distracted, scattered, and destroyed, so that they could not reach the Power of God. At which the poor Soul was still more afraid, and began to pray more earnestly. But the Devil with his Desire took hold of the Mercurial kindled fiery Wheel of Life, and awakened the evil Properties, so that evil or false Inclinations arose in the Soul, and went into that Thing wherein they had taken most Pleasure and Delight before.

The poor Soul would very fain go forward to God with its Will, and therefore used all its Endeavors; but its Thoughts continually fled away from God into earthly Things, and could not go to Him.

Upon this the Soul sighed and bewailed itself to God; but it seemed as if it were quite forsaken by Him, and cast out from His Presence. It could not get so much as one Look of Grace, but was in mere Anguish, Fear and Terror, and dreaded every Moment that the Wrath and severe Judgment of God would be manifested in it, and that the Devil would take hold of it and have it. And thereupon the Soul fell into such great Heaviness, and Sorrow, that it became weary of all the temporal Things, which before had been its chief Joy and Happiness. The earthly natural Will indeed desired those Things still, but the Soul would willingly leave them altogether, and desired to die to all temporal Lust and Joy whatsoever, and longed only after its first Native Country, from whence it originally came. But the Soul found itself to be far from thence, in great

Distress and Want, and knew not what to do, yet resolved to enter into itself, and try to pray more earnestly.

The Devil's Opposition: But the Devil opposed it, and withheld it so that it could not bring itself into any greater Fervency of Repentance.

He awakened the old earthly Lusts in its Heart, that they might still keep their evil Nature and false Right therein, and set them at Variance with the newborn Will and Desire of the Soul. For they would not die to their own Will and Light, but would still maintain their temporal Pleasures, and so kept the poor Soul captive in their evil Desires, that it could not stir, though it sighed and longed even more after the Grace of God. For whenever it prayed, or offered to press forward towards God, then the Lusts of the Flesh swallowed up the Rays and Ejaculations that went forth from it, and brought them away from God into earthly Thoughts, that it might not partake of Divine Strength. Which caused the poor Soul to think itself forsaken of God, not knowing that He was so near it and did thus attract it. Also the Devil got access to it, and entered into the fiery Mercury, or fiery Wheel of its Life, and mingled his Desires with the earthly Lusts of the Flesh, and tempted the poor Soul; saying to it in the earthly Thoughts, *"Why do you pray? Do you think that God knows you or regards you: Consider but what Thoughts you have in His Presence; are they not altogether evil? You have no Faith or Belief in God at all; how then should He hear you? He hears you not, leave off; why will you needlessly torment and vex yourself? You has Time enough to repent at Leisure. Will you be mad? Do but look upon the World, I pray you, a little; does it not live in Jollity and Mirth? Yet it will be saved well enough for that. Has not Christ paid the Ransom and satisfied all Men? You need only persuade and comfort yourself that it is done for you, and then you shall be saved. You cannot possibly in this World come to any Feeling of God; therefore leave off, and take care for your Body, and look after temporal Glory. What do you suppose will become of you, if you turn to be so stupid and melancholy? You will be the Scorn of everybody, and they will laugh at your Folly; and so you will spend your Days in mere Sorrow and Heaviness, which is pleasing neither to God nor Nature. I pray you, look upon the Beauty of the World; for God has created and placed you in it, to be a Lord over all Creatures, and to rule them. Gather a Store of temporal Goods beforehand, that you may not be beholden to the World, or stand in Need hereafter. And when Old Age cometh, or when you grow near your End, then there will be Time enough to prepare yourself for Repentance. God will save you, and receive you into the heavenly Mansions then. There is no need of such ado in vexing, bewailing, and stirring up yourself, as you make."*

The Condition of the Soul: In these and the like Thoughts the Soul was ensnared by the Devil, and brought into the Lusts of the Flesh, and earthly Desires; and so was bound as if it were with Fetters and strong Chains, so that it did not know what to do. It looked back a little into the World and the Pleasures thereof, but still felt in itself a Hunger after the Divine Grace, and would always rather enter into Repentance, and Favor with God. For the Hand of God had touched and bruised the Soul, and therefore it could nowhere find Rest; but always sighed within itself in Sorrow for the Sins it had committed, and longed to be rid of them. Yet it could not get true Repentance, or even the Knowledge of Sin, though it had a mighty Hunger and longing Desire after such penitential Sorrow.

The Soul being thus heavy and sad, and finding no Remedy or Rest, began to cast about where it might find a fit Place to perform true Repentance in, where it might be free from Business, Hindrances and Cares of the World; and also by what Means it might win the Favor of God. And at length it decided to take itself to some private solitary Place, and give up all worldly Employments and temporal Things; and hoped, that by being bountiful and pitiful to the Poor, it should obtain God's Mercy. Thus did it devise all Kinds of Ways to get Rest, and gain the Love, Favor, and Grace of God again. But all that it tried would not do; for its worldly Business still followed it in the Lusts of the Flesh, and it was ensnared in the Net of the Devil now, as well as before, and could not attain Rest. And though for a little while it was somewhat cheered with earthly Things, yet presently it fell to be as sad and heavy again, as it was before. The Truth was, it felt the awakened Wrath of God in itself, but knew not how that came to pass, nor what ailed it. For many Times great Trouble and Terror fell upon it, which made it comfortless, sick, and faint with Fear; so mightily did the first bruising Ray or Influence of the stirring Grace work upon it. And yet it knew not that Christ was in the Wrath and severe Justice of God, and fought therein with Satan, that Spirit of Error, which was incorporated in the Soul and its Body; nor it understood not that the Hunger and Desire to turn and repent came from Christ Himself, by which it was drawn in this Manner; neither did it know what hindered it from Attaining to Divine Feeling. It knew not that itself was a Monster, and did bear the Image of the Serpent, in which the Devil had such Power and Access to it, and had confounded all its good Desires, Thoughts, and Motions, and brought them away from God and Goodness; concerning which Christ Himself had said,

"The Devil snatches the Word out of their Hearts, lest they should believe and be saved."

An enlightened and regenerate Soul met the distressed Soul: By the Providence of God, an enlightened and regenerate Soul met this poor afflicted and distressed Soul, and said, "What ails you, you distressed Soul, that you are so restless and troubled?"

The distressed Soul answered: The Creator has hid His Countenance from me, so that I cannot come to His Rest; therefore I am thus troubled, and know not what I shall do to get His Lovingkindness again. For I feel as though great Cliffs and Rocks lie in my Way to His grace, so that I cannot come to Him. Though I sigh and long after Him ever so much, yet I am kept back so that I cannot partake of His Power, Virtue and Strength.

The enlightened Soul said: You bear the monstrous Shape of the Devil, and are clothed therewith; in which, being his own Property or Principle, he has Access or Power of Entrance into you, and thereby keeps your Will from penetrating into God. For if your Will might penetrate into God, it would be anointed with the highest Power and Strength of God, in the Resurrection of our Lord Jesus Christ; and that Unction would break in Pieces the Monster which you carry about within you; and your first Image of Paradise would revive in the Center; which would destroy the Devil's Power therein, and you would become as an Angel again. And because the Devil envies you this Happiness, he holds you captive in his Desire in the Lusts of the Flesh; from which if you are not delivered, you will be separated from God, and can never enter into our Society.

The distressed Soul terrified: At this Speech the poor distressed Soul was so terrified and amazed, that it could not speak one Word more. When it found that it stood in the Form and Condition of the Serpent, which separated it from God; and that the Devil was so near to it in that Condition, who injected evil Thoughts into the Will of the Soul, and had so much Power over it thereby, that it was near Damnation, and sticking fast in the Abyss or bottomless Pit of Hell, in the Anger of God; it would have even given up any hope for the Divine Mercy; except for the Power, Virtue and Strength of the first Stirring of the Grace of God, which had before bruised the Soul; this upheld and preserved it from total Despair. But still it wrestled in itself between Hope and Doubt; whatsoever Hope built up was thrown down again by Doubt. And thus was it agitated with such continual Disquiet, that at last the World and all the Glory thereof became loathsome to it, neither would it enjoy worldly Pleasures anymore; and yet for all this, it could not come to Rest.

The enlightened Soul came again, and spoke to the troubled Soul: On a Time the enlightened Soul came again to this Soul, and finding it still in so great Trouble, Anguish and Grief of Mind, said to it:

What do you? Will you destroy yourself in your Anguish and Sorrow? Why do you torment yourself in your OWN Power and Will, who are but a Worm, seeing your Torment increases thereby more and more? Yea, if you should sink yourself down to the Bottom of the Sea, or could fly to the uttermost Coasts of the Morning, or raise yourself above the Stars, yet you would not be released. For the more you grieve, torment, and trouble yourself, the more painful your Nature will be; and yet you will not be able to come to any Rest. For your Power is quite lost; and as a dry Stick burnt to a Coal cannot grow green and spring afresh by its OWN Power, nor get Sap to flourish again with other Trees and Plants, so neither can you reach the Place of God by your OWN Power and Strength, and transform yourself into that Angelical Image which you had at first. For in respect to God you are withered and dry, like a dead Plant that has lost its Sap and Strength, and so are become a dry tormenting Hunger. Your Properties are like Heat and Cold, which continually strive one against the other, and can never unite.

The distressed Soul said: What then shall I do to bud forth again, and recover the first Life, wherein I was at Rest before I became an Image?

The enlightened Soul said: You should do Nothing at all but forsake your OWN Will, viz. that which you call *I*, or your *Self*. By which Means all your evil Properties will grow weak, faint, and ready to die; and then you will sink down again into that One Thing, from which you are originally sprung. For now you lie captive in the Creatures; but if your Will forsakes them, the Creatures, with their evil Inclinations, will die in you, which at present stay and hinder you so that you cannot come to God. But if you take this Course, your God will meet you with His infinite Love, which He has manifested in Christ Jesus in the Humanity, or Human Nature. And that will impart Sap, Life, and Vigor to you; whereby you may bud, spring, and flourish again, and rejoice in the Living God, as a Branch growing on His True Vine. And so you will at length recover the Image of God, and be delivered from the Image or Condition of the Serpent: Then shall you come to be my Brother, and have Fellowship with the Angels.

The poor Soul said: How can I forsake my Will, so that the Creatures which lodge therein may die, seeing I must be in the World, and also have need of it as long as I live?

The enlightened Soul said: Now you have worldly Power and Riches, which you possesses as your OWN, to do what you will with, and regard not how you get or use the same; employing them in the Service and Indulgence of your OWN carnal and vain Desires. Nay, though you see the poor and needy Wretch, who wants your Help, and is your Brother, yet you help him not, but lay heavy Burdens upon him, by requiring more of him than his Abilities will bear, or his Necessities afford; and oppress him, by forcing him to spend his Labor and Sweat for you, and for the Gratification of your voluptuous Will. You are moreover proud, and insult over him, and behave roughly and sternly to him, exalting yourself above him, and making small Account of him in Respect to yourself. Then that poor oppressed Brother of yours cometh, and complains with Sighs towards God, that he cannot reap the Benefit of his Labor and Pains, but is forced by you to live in Misery. By which Sighings and Groanings of his, he raises up the Wrath of God in you; which makes your Flame and Unquietness still the greater. These are the Creatures which you are in Love with, and have broken yourself off from God for their Sakes, and brought your Love into them, or them into your Love, so that they live therein. You nourish and keep them by continually receiving them into your Desire, for they live in and by your receiving them into your Mind; because you thereby bring the Lust of your Life into them. They are but unclean, filthy, and evil Births, and Issues of the bestial Nature, which yet, by your receiving them in your Lust or Desire, have gotten an Image, and formed themselves in you. And that Image is a Beast with four Heads; *First*, Pride. *Secondly*, Covetousness. *Thirdly*, Envy. *Fourthly*, Anger. And in these four Properties the Foundation of Hell consists, which you carry in you and about you. It is imprinted and engraven in you, and you are wholly taken

Captive thereby. For these Properties live in your natural Life; and thereby you are severed or cut off from God, neither can you ever come to Him, unless you so forsake these evil Creatures that they may die in you.

But since you desire me to tell you how to forsake your own perverse creaturely Will so that the Creatures in you might die, and how yet you might live along with them in the World, I must assure you that there is but one Way to do it, which is narrow and straight, and will be very hard and irksome to you at the Beginning, but afterwards you will walk in it cheerfully.

You must seriously consider, that in the Course of this worldly Life you walk in the Anger of God and in the Foundation of Hell; and that this is not your true Native Country; but that a True Christian should, and must live in Christ, and in his Walking truly follow Him; and that he cannot be a True Christian, unless the Spirit and Power of Christ so live in him, that he becomes wholly Subject to It. Now seeing the Kingdom of Christ is not of this World, but in Heaven, therefore you must always be in a continual Ascension towards Heaven, if you will follow Christ; though your Body must dwell among the Creatures and use them.

The narrow Way to which perpetual Ascension into Heaven and Imitation of Christ is this: You must despair of all your OWN Power and Strength, for in and by your OWN Power you cannot reach the Gates of God; and firmly purpose and resolve wholly to give yourself up to the Mercy of God, and to sink down with your whole Mind and Reason into the Passion and Death of our Lord Jesus Christ, always desiring to persevere in the same, and to die from all your Creatures therein. Also you must resolve to watch and guard your Mind, Thoughts and

Inclinations that they admit no Evil into them, neither must you suffer yourself to be held fast by temporal Honor or Profit. You must resolve likewise to put away from you all Unrighteousness, and whatsoever else may hinder the Freedom of your Motion and Progress. Your Will must be wholly pure, and fixed in a firm Resolution never to return to its old Idols any more, but that you will leave them the very Instant they are known to you, and separate your Mind from them, and enter into the sincere Way of Truth and Righteousness, according to the plain and full Doctrine of Christ. And as you do thus purpose to forsake the Enemies of your own inward Nature, so also must you forgive all your outward Enemies, and resolve to meet them with your Love; so that there may be left no Creature, Person, or Thing at all able to take hold of your Will and captivate it; but that it may be sincere, and purged from all Creatures. Nay further; if it should be required, you must be willing and ready to forsake all your temporal Honor and Profit for Christ's sake, and regard nothing that is Earthly so as to set your Heart and Affections upon it; but esteem yourself in whatsoever State, Degree, and Condition you are, as to worldly Rank or Riches, to be but a Servant of God and of your Fellow-Christians; or as a Steward in the Office wherein your Lord has placed you. All Arrogance and Self-Exaltation must be humbled, brought low, and so annihilated that nothing of your OWN or of any other Creature may stay in your Will to bring your Thoughts or Imagination to be set upon it.

You must also firmly impress it on your Mind, that you shall certainly partake of the promised Grace in the Merit of Jesus Christ, viz. of His outflowing Love, which indeed is already in you, and which will deliver you from your Creatures, and enlighten your Will, and kindle it with the

Flame of Love, whereby you shall have Victory over the Devil. Not as if you could will or do anything in your OWN Strength, but only enter into the Suffering and Resurrection of Jesus Christ, and take them to yourself, and with them assault and break in Pieces the Kingdom of the Devil in you, and mortify your Creatures. You must resolve to enter into this Way this very Hour, and never to depart from it, but willingly to submit yourself to God in all your Endeavors and Doings, that He may do with you what He pleases.

When your Will is thus prepared and resolved, it has then broken through its own Creatures, and is sincere in the Presence of God, and clothed with the merits of Jesus Christ. It may then freely go to the Father with the Prodigal Son, and fall down in His Presence and pour forth its Prayers; and putting forth all its Strength in this Divine Work, confess its Sins Disobedience; and how far it has departed from God. This must be done not with bare Words, but with all its Strength, which indeed amounts only to a strong Purpose and Resolution; for the Soul of itself has no Strength or Power to effect any good Work.

Now when you are thus ready, and that your Heavenly Father shall see your coming and returning to Him in such Repentance and Humility, He will inwardly speak to you, and say in you, *"Behold this is My Son which I had lost; he was dead and is alive again."* And He will come and meet you in your Mind with the Grace and Love of Jesus Christ, and embrace you with the Beams of His Love, and kiss you with His Spirit and Strength; and then you shall receive Grace to pour out your Confession before Him, and to pray powerfully. This indeed is the right Place where you must wrestle in the Light of His Countenance. And if you stand resolutely here, and do not shrink back, you shall see or feel great Wonders. For you shall find

Christ in you assaulting Hell, and crushing your Beasts in Pieces, and that a great Tumult and Misery will arise in you; also your secret undiscovered Sins will then first awake, and labor to separate you from God, and to keep you back. Thus shall you truly find and feel how Death and Life fight one against the other, and shall understand by what passes within yourself, what Heaven and Hell are. At which Time be not moved, but stand firm and shrink not; for at length all your Creatures will grow faint, weak, and ready to die; and then your Will shall wax stronger, and be able to subdue and keep down the evil Inclinations. So shall your Will and Mind ascend into Heaven every day, and your Creatures gradually die away. You will get a Mind wholly new, and begin to be a new Creature, and getting rid of the Bestial deformity, recover the Divine Image. Thus shall you be delivered from your present Anguish, and return to your Original Rest.

The poor Soul's Practice: Then the poor Soul began to practice this Course with such Earnestness, that it conceived it should get the Victory presently; but it found that the Gates of Heaven were shut against it in its own Strength and Power and it was as if it were rejected and forsaken by God, and received not so much as one Look or Glimpse of Grace from Him. Upon which it said to itself, *"Surely you have not sincerely submitted yourself to God. Desire Nothing at all of Him, but only submit yourself to His Judgment and Condemnation, that He may kill your evil Inclinations. Sink down into Him beyond the Limits of Nature and Creature, and submit yourself to Him, that He may do with you what He will, for you are not worthy to speak to Him."* Accordingly the Soul took a Resolution to sink down, and to forsake its own Will; and when it had done so, there fell upon it presently the greatest Repentance that could be for the Sins it had committed; and it bewailed bitterly its ugly Shape, and was truly and deeply sorry that the evil Creatures did dwell within it. And because of its Sorrow it could not speak one more Word in the Presence of God, but began in its Repentance to realize the bitter Passion and Death of Jesus Christ, viz. what great Anguish and Torment He had suffered for its Sake, in order to deliver it out of its Anguish, and change it into the Image of God. In which Consideration it wholly sunk down, and did Nothing but complain of its Ignorance and Negligence, and that it had not been thankful to its Redeemer, nor once considered the great Love He had shown to it, but had idly spent its Time, and not at all regarded how it might come to partake of His purchased and proffered Grace; but instead thereof had formed in itself the Images and Figures of earthly Things, with the vain Lusts and Pleasures of the World. Whereby it had gotten such bestial Inclinations, that now it must lie captive in great Misery, and for very shame dared not lift up its Eyes to God, Who hid the Light of His Countenance from it, and would not so much as look upon it. And as it was thus sighing and crying, it was drawn into the Abyss or Pit of Horror, and laid itself as it were at the Gates of Hell, there to perish. Upon which the poor troubled Soul was as it were bereft of Sense, and wholly forsaken, so that it in a Manner forgot all its Doings, and would willingly yield itself to Death, and cease to be a Creature. Accordingly it did yield itself to Death, and desired Nothing else but to die and perish in the Death of its Redeemer, Jesus Christ, Who had suffered such Torments and Death for its Sake. And in this Perishing it began to sigh and pray in itself very inwardly to the Divine Goodness, and to sink down into the mere Mercy of God.

Upon this there suddenly appeared unto it the amiable Countenance of the Love of God, which penetrated through it as a great Light, and made it exceedingly joyful. It then began to pray aright, and to thank the Most High for such Grace, and to rejoice abundantly, that it was delivered from the Death and Anguish of Hell. Now it tasted of the Sweetness of God, and of His promised Truth; and now all the evil Spirits, which had harassed it before, and kept it back from the Grace, Love, and inward Presence of God, were forced to depart from it. The "Wedding of the Lamb" was now kept and solemnized, that is, the Noble Sophia [or the Eternal Wisdom] espoused or betrothed herself to the Soul; and the Seal-Ring of Christ's Victory was impressed into its Essence, and it was received to be a Child and Heir of God again.

When this was done, the Soul became very joyful, and began to work in this new Power, and to celebrate with Praise the Wonders of God, and thought thenceforth to walk continually in the same Light, Strength, and Joy. But it was soon assaulted; from without, by the Shame and Reproach of the World, and from within, by great Temptation, so that it began to doubt whether its Ground was truly from God, and whether it had really partaken of His Grace. For the Accuser, Satan, went to it, and would fain lead it out of this Course, and make it doubtful whether it was the true Way; whispering thus to it inwardly: *"This happy Change in your Spirit is not from God, but only from your own Imagination."* Also the Divine Light retired in the Soul, and shone but in the inward Ground, as Fire raked up in Embers, so that Reason was perplexed, and thought itself forsaken, and the Soul knew not what had happened to itself, nor whether it had really and truly tasted of the heavenly Gift or not. Yet it could not leave off struggling; for the burning Fire of Love was sown in it, which had raised in it a vehement and continual Hunger and Thirst after Divine Sweetness. So at length it began to pray aright, and to humble itself in the Presence of God, and to examine and try its evil Inclinations and Thoughts and to put them away. By which means the Will of its Reason was broken, and the evil Inclinations inherent in it were killed and extirpated more and more. This Process was very severe and painful to the Nature of the Body, for it made it faint and weak, as if it had been very sick; and yet it was no natural Sickness that it had, but only the Melancholy of its earthly Nature which was feeling and lamenting the Destruction of its evil Lusts.

Now when the earthly Reason found itself thus forsaken, and the poor Soul saw that it was despised outwardly, and derided by the World, because it would no longer walk in the Way of Wickedness and Vanity; and also that it was inwardly assaulted by the Accuser, Satan, who mocked it, and continually set before it the Beauty, Riches, and Glory of the World, and called it a Fool for not embracing them; it began to think and say thus within itself; *"O eternal God! What shall I now do to come to Rest?"*

The enlightened Soul met it again, and spoke to it: While it was in this Consideration, the enlightened Soul met with it again, and said, "What ails you, my Brother, that you are so heavy and sad?"

The distressed Soul said: I have followed your Counsel, and thereby attained a Ray, or Emanation of the Divine Sweetness, but it is gone from me again. and I am now deserted. Moreover I have outwardly very great Trials and Afflictions in the World; for all my good Friends forsake and scorn me; and am also inwardly assaulted with Anguish and Doubt, and know not what to do.

The enlightened Soul said: Now I like you very well; for now our beloved Lord Jesus Christ is performing that same Pilgrimage or Process on Earth with you and in you, which He did Himself when He was in this World, Who was continually reviled, despised, and evil spoken of and had nothing of His own in it; and now you bear His Mark or Badge. But do not wonder at it, or think it strange; for it must be so, in order that you may be tried, refined, and purified. In this Anguish and Distress you will necessarily hunger and cry after Deliverance; and by such Hunger and Prayer you will attract Grace to you both from within and from without. For you must grow from above and from beneath to be the Image of God again. Just as a young Plant is agitated by the Wind, and must stand its Ground in Heat and Cold, drawing Strength and Virtue to it from above and from beneath by that Agitation, and must endure many a Tempest, and undergo much Danger before it can come to be a Tree, and bring forth Fruit. For through that Agitation the Virtue of the Sun moves in the Plant, whereby its wild Properties come to be penetrated and tinctured with the Solar Virtue, and grow thereby.

And this is the Time wherein you must play the Part of a valiant Soldier in the Spirit of Christ, and cooperate yourself Therewith. For now the Eternal Father by His fiery Power begets His Son in you, who changes the Fire of the Father, namely, the first Principle, or wrathful Property of the Soul, into the Flame of Love, so that out of Fire and Light (viz. Wrath and Love) there comes to be ONE Essence, Being, or Substance, which is the true Temple of God. And now you shall bud forth out of the Vine Christ, in the Vineyard of God, and bring forth Fruit in your Life, and by assisting and instructing others, show forth your Love in Abundance, as a good Tree. For Paradise must thus spring up again in you, through the

Wrath of God, and Hell be changed into Heaven in you. Therefore be not dismayed at the Temptations of the Devil, who seeks and strives for the Kingdom, which he once had in you; but having now lost it, he must be confounded, and depart from you. And he covers you outwardly with the Shame and Reproach of the World, that his own Shame may not be known, and that you may be hidden to the World. For with your new Birth or regenerated Nature, you are in the Divine Harmony in Heaven. Be patient, therefore, and wait upon the Lord; and whatsoever shall befall you, take it all from His Hands, as intended by Him for your highest Good. And so the enlightened Soul departed from it.

The distressed Soul's Course: The distressed soul began its Course now under the patient Suffering of Christ, and depending solely upon the Strength and Power of God in it, entered into Hope. Thenceforth it grew stronger every Day, and its evil Inclinations died more and more in it. So that it arrived at length to a High State or Degree of Grace; and the Gates of the Divine Revelation and the Kingdom of Heaven, were opened to, and manifested in it. And thus the Soul through Repentance, Faith, and Prayer, returned to its Original and True Rest, and became a Right and Beloved Child of God again; to which may He of His Infinite Mercy help us all. Amen. "But you are a chosen Generation, a royal Priesthood, a holy Nation, a peculiar People; that you should show forth the Praises of Him Who has called you out of Darkness into His marvelous Light."

VI. THE SIGNATURE OF ALL THINGS

Chapter VII

32. Now it behooves the wise Seeker to consider the whole Process with the Humanity of Christ from his Opening in the Womb of his Mother Mary, even to his Resurrection and Ascension; and so he may well find the Feast of Pentecost with the Joyful Spirit, wherewith he may tincture, cure, and heal whatever is broken and destroyed: We declare it in the Ground of Truth, as we have highly known it; for the Rose in the Time of the Lily shall blossom in May when the Winter is past, for Blindness to the Wicked, and for Light to the Seeing.

33. God be forever praised, who has granted us Eyes to see through the poisonous Spring or the Heart of the Basilisk, and see the Day of Restitution of all whatever *Adam* lost.

34. Now we will come to the Process of Christ, and go with him out of Eternity into Time, and out of Time into Eternity, and bring again the Wonders of Time into Eternity, and openly set forth the Pearl, for Honour unto Christ, and Scorn to the Devil; he that sleeps is blind, but he that wakes sees what the May brings.

35. Christ said, *Seek, and you shall find, knock, and it shall be opened unto you*: You know that Christ signifies in a Parable concerning the wounded Samaritan, that he fell among Murderers, who beat him and wounded him, and pulled off his Clothes, and went away, and left him half dead, till the Samaritan came, and took Pity on him,

dressed him, and poured Oil into his Wounds, and brought him into the Inn: This is a manifest and lively Representation of the Corruption of Man in Paradise, and also of the Corruption of the Earth in the Curse of God, when Paradise departed from it.

36. Now wilt thou be a *Magus*? Then thou must become the Samaritan, otherwise thou canst not heal the wounded and decayed; for the Body which thou must heal is half dead, and sorely wounded, also its right Garment is torn off, so that it is very hard for thee to know the Man whom thou wilt heal, unless thou hast the Eyes and Will of the Samaritan, and seekest nothing else thereby but to restore the Loss of the Wounded.

73. Therefore if the *Magus* will seek Paradise in the Curse of the Earth, and find it, then must he first walk in the Person of Christ; God must be manifest in him, understand in the internal Man, that he may have the magical Sight: He must deal with his Purpose as the World did with Christ, and then he may find Paradise, wherein is no Death.

74. But if he be not in this Birth of Restoration, and walks not himself in the Way wherein Christ walked upon the Earth, if he steps not forth into the Will and Spirit of Christ, then let him give over and leave off his Seeking; he finds nothing but Death, and the Curse of God. I tell him plainly and faithfully, for the Pearl of which I write is paradisical, which God does not cast before Swine, but gives it to his Children for their Play and Delight.

75. And though much Might be mentioned here, that even Reason Might obtain open Eyes, yet it is not to be done; for the wicked would grow worse, and more full of Pride; therefore seeing he is not worthy of Paradise, and also cannot enter thereinto, no heavenly Jewel shall be given

him: And therefore God hides it, and permits him to whom he reveals it, to speak of it no otherwise than magically; therefore no one attains it, unless he himself be a *Magus* in Christ, unless Paradise be manifest in his internal Man; and then he may find, if he be born to it, and chosen by God.

Chapter XVI

Concerning the eternal Signature *and* heavenly Joy; *why all things were brought into* Evil *and Good*

1. The Creation of the whole Creation is Nothing else but a Manifestation of the all-essential, unsearchable God; all whatever he is in his eternal unbeginning Generation and Dominion, of that is also the Creation, but not in the Omnipotence and Power, but like an Apple which grows upon the Tree, which is not the Tree itself, but grows from the Power of the Tree: Even so all Things are sprung forth out of the divine Desire, and created into an Essence, where in the Beginning there was no such Essence present, but only that same Mystery of the eternal Generation, in which there has been an eternal perfection.

2. For God has not brought forth the Creation, that he should be thereby perfect, but for his own Manifestation, *viz.* for the great Joy and Glory; not that this Joy first began with the Creation, no, for it was from Eternity in the great Mystery, yet only as a Spiritual Melody and Sport in itself.

3. The Creation is the same Sport out of himself, *viz.* a Platform or Instrument of the Eternal Spirit, with which he melodises: and it is even as a great Harmony of manifold Instruments which are all tuned into one Harmony; for the eternal Word, or divine Sound or Voice, which is a Spirit, has introduced itself with the Generation

of the great Mystery into Formings, *viz.* into an expressed Word or Sound: And as the Joyful Melody is in itself in the Spirit of the eternal Generation, so likewise is the Instrument, *viz.* the expressed Form in itself, which the living eternal Voice guides, and strikes with his own eternal Will-Spirit, that it Sounds and melodises; as an Organ of divers and various Sounds or Notes is moved with one only Air, so that each Note, yea every Pipe has its peculiar Tune, and yet there is but one Manner of Air or Breath in all Notes, which Sounds in each Note or Pipe according as the Instrument or Organ is made.

4. Thus in the Eternity there is only one Spirit in the whole Work of the divine Manifestation, which is the Manifestator in the expressed Voice and also in the speaking Voice of God, which is the Life of the grand Mystery, and of all that is generated from thence; he is the Manifestator of all the Works of God.

5. All the Angelical Kingdoms are as a prepared Work, *viz.* a Manifestation of the eternal Sound of the Voice of God, and are as a particularity out of the great Mystery, and yet are only one in the divine eternal speaking Word, Sound, or Voice of God; for one only Spirit rules them; each Angelical prince is a Property out of the Voice of God, and bears the great Name of God; as we have a Type and Figure of it in the Stars of the Firmament, and in the Kingdoms and Dominions upon the Earth among all Generations, where every Lord bears his high Title, respective Name and Office: So likewise do the Stars in the Firmament, which are altogether one only Dominion in Power under them, where the great Stars bear the Name and the Office of the Forms in the Mystery of the seven Properties, and the other after them, as a particularity of Houses or Divisions, where every one is a peculiar Harmony or Operation, like a Kingdom, and yet all

proceeds in one Harmony; like a Clock-Work, which is entirely composed in itself, and all the pieces Work mutually together in one; and yet the great fixed Stars keep their peculiar Property in the Essence of Operation, especially the seven Planets according to the seven Properties of Nature, as an under Pregnatress of the eternal Mystery, or as an Instrument of the Spirit out of the eternal Mystery.

6. This Birth of the *Astrum* begets in the four Elements, *viz.* in its Body or Essence, Joy and Sorrow, and all is very good in itself; only the Alteration of the Creature proceeds from the lustful Imagination, whereby the Creature elevates the Wrath of the Fire in the Properties, and brings them forth out of the Likeness of their Accord: Nothing is evil which remains in the equal Accord; for that which the Worst causes and makes with its coming forth out of the Accord, that likewise the Best makes in the equal Accord; that which there makes Sorrow, that makes also in the Likeness Joy; therefore no Creature can blame its Creator, as if he made it evil; all was very exceeding good; but with its own Elevation and Departure out of the Likeness it becomes evil, and brings itself out of the Form [or Property] of the Love and Joy, into a painful tormenting Form and Property.

7. King Lucifer stood in the Beginning of his Creation in highest Joyfulness, but he departed from the Likeness, and put himself forth out of the Accord [or heavenly Concert] into the cold, dark, fiery Generation, out of which the hot fiery Generation arises; he forsook his Order, and went out of the Harmony, wherein God created him; he would be Lord over all, and so he entered into the austere Fire's domination, and is now an Instrument in the austere Fire's Might, upon which also the all-essential Spirit strikes and Sounds upon his

Instrument, but it Sounds only according to the wrathful Fire's Property: as the Harmony, *viz.* the Life's-Form is in each Thing, so is also the Sound or Tone of the eternal Voice therein; in the Holy [it is] holy, in the Perverse it is perverse: All Things must praise the Creator of all Beings; the Devils praise him in the Might of Wrath, and the Angels and Men praise him in the Might of Love.

8. The Being of all Beings is but one only Being, but in its Generation it separates itself into two Principles, *viz.* into Light and Darkness, into Joy and Sorrow, into Evil and Good, into Love and Anger, into Fire and Light, and out of these two eternal Beginnings [or Principles] into the third Beginning, *viz.* into the Creation, to its own Love-Play and Melody, according to the Property of both eternal Desires.

9. Thus each Thing goes into its Harmony, and is guided [or driven] by one only Spirit, which is in each Thing according to the Property of the Thing; and this is the Clock [or Watch-Work] of the great Mystery of Eternity in each Principle according to the Property of the Principle, and then according to the innate Form of the composed Instrument of the same Creatures, even in all these Beginnings [or Principles].

10. Death is the Bound-Mark of all whatever is temporal, whereby the Evil may be destroyed; but that which arises out of the eternal Beginnings, and in its Harmony and Life's-Form enters into another Figure, that departs out of God's Harmony, out of the true Order wherein God created it, and is cast out of the same Harmony into its Likeness, as a dissonant discording Melody or Sound in the great excellent well-tuned Harmony; for it is an opposite contrary Thing, and bears another Tone, Sound, and Will, and so it is introduced into its Likeness; and

therefore Hell is given to the Devil for his House and Habitation, because he introduced his Life's-Form into the Anger of God, and into the fiery Wrath of the eternal Nature, so that now he is the Instrument in the eternal Fire of God, and the Anger-Spirit strikes his Instrument, and yet it must stand to the Honour and Admiration of God, and be the Sport and Play in the Desire and Property of the wrathful Anger.

11. The Anger and Wrath of God are now his Joy, not as if he feared, sorrowed, and lived in Impotency; no, but in great Strength and fiery Might, as a potent King and Lord, yet only in the same Property of which he himself is, *viz.* in the first Principle in the dark World.

12. The like also we are to know concerning the Angelical World, *viz.* the second Principle, where God's Light and glorious Beauty shine in every Being [or Thing], and the divine Voice or Sound rises up in all Creatures in great Joyfulness; where the Spirit proceeding from the divine Voice makes a Joyfulness, and an incessant continual Love-Desire in those Creatures, and in all the divine Angelical Beings: As there is an Anguish-Source and trembling in the painful Fire, so in like Manner there is a trembling Joyfulness in the Light and Love-Fire, *viz.* a great Elevation of the Voice of God, which makes in the Angels and in the like Creatures, as the Souls of Men, a great Manifestation of the divine Joyfulness.

13. The Voice [or breath] of God continually and eternally brings forth its Joy through the Creature, as through an Instrument; the Creature is the Manifestation of the Voice of God: What God is in the eternal Generation of his eternal Word out of the great Mystery of the Father's Property, that the Creature is in the Image

as a joyful Harmony, wherewith the Eternal Spirit plays or melodises.

14. All Properties of the great eternal Mystery of the Pregnatress of all Beings are manifest in the holy Angelical and humane Creatures; and we are not to think thereof, as if the Creatures only stood still and rejoiced at the Glory of God, and admired only in Joy; not, but it is as the Eternal Spirit of God works from Eternity to Eternity in the great Mystery of the divine Generation, and continually manifests the infinite and numberless Wisdom of God; even as the Earth brings forth always fair Blossoms, Herbs, and Trees, so also Metals and all Manner of Beings, and puts them forth sometimes more sovereign, powerful, and fair, than at other Times; and as one arises in the Essence, another falls down, and there is an incessant lasting Enjoyment and Labour.

15. Thus likewise is the eternal Generation of the holy Mystery in great Power and Reprocreation [or paradisical Pullulation] where one divine Fruit of the great Love-Desire stands with another in the divine Essence; and all is as a continual Love-combat or wrestling Delight; a Blooming of fair Colours, and a pleasant ravishing Smell of the divine *Mercury*, according to the divine Nature's Property, a continual good Taste of Love from the divine Desire.

16. Of all whatever this World is an earthly Type and Resemblance, that is in the divine Kingdom in great Perfection in the Spiritual Essence; not only Spirit, as a Will, or Thought, but Essence, corporeal Essence, Sap and Power; but as incomprehensible in reference to the outward World: For this visible World was generated and created out of the same spiritual Essence in which the pure Element is; and also out of the dark Essence in the

Mystery of the Wrath (Being the Original of the eternal manifest Essence from whence the Properties arise) as an out-spoken Breath out of the Being of all Beings: Not that it was made of the eternal Essence, but out of the breathing forth or [expression] of the eternal Essence; out of Love and Anger, out of Evil and Good, as a peculiar Generation of a peculiar Principle in the Hand of the Eternal Spirit.

17. Therefore all whatever is in this World is a Type and Figure of the Angelical World: not that the Evil, which is alike manifest with the Good in this World, is also manifest in Heaven; no, they are separated into two Principles; in Heaven all is Good which is Evil in Hell; whatever is Anguish and torment in Hell, that is Good and a Joy in Heaven; for there all stands in the Light's Source; and in Hell all stands in the Wrath in the dark Source.

18. Hell, *viz.* the dark World has also its Generation of Fruits; and there is even such an Essence and Dominion in them as in Heaven, but in Nature and Manner of the wrathful Property; for the fiery Property makes all Evil in the Darkness, and in the Light it makes all Things good; and in Sum, all is wholly one in both eternal Worlds; but Light and Darkness separates them, so that they stand as an eternal Enmity opposite one to another, to the End that it may be known what is Evil or Good, Joy or Sorrow, Love or Anger: There is only a Distinction between the Love-Desire of the Light, and the Anger-Desire of the Darkness.

19. In the Original of the eternal Nature, in the Father's Property in the great Mystery of all Beings, it is wholly one: for the same only Fire is even in the Angelical World, but in another Source, *viz.* a Love-Fire, which is a Poison, and a Fire of Anger to the Devils, and to Hell; for

the Love-Fire is a Death, Mortification, and an Enmity of the Anger-Fire; it deprives the Wrath of its Might, and this the Wrath wills not, and it also cannot be; for if there were no Wrath, there would be no Fire, and also no Light: If the eternal Wrath were not, the eternal Joy also would not be; in the Light the Wrath is changed into Joy; the wrathful Fire's Essence is mortified as to the Darkness in the wrathful Fire, and out of the same Dying the Light and Love-Fire arise; as the Light burns forth from the Candle, and yet in the Candle the Fire and Light are but one Thing.

20. Thus also the great Mystery of all Beings is in the Eternity in itself only one Thing, but in its Explication and Manifestation it goes from Eternity to Eternity into two Essences, *viz.* into Evil and good; what is Evil to one Thing, that is Good to another. Hell is Evil to the Angels, for they were not created thereunto; but it is Good to the Hellish Creatures: So also Heaven is Evil to the Hellish Creatures, for it is their Poison and Death, an eternal Dying, and an eternal Captivity.

21. Therefore there is an eternal Enmity, and God is only called God according to the Light of his Love; he is indeed himself all, but according to the Darkness he saith, *I am an angry jealous God, and a consuming* Fire.

22. Every Creature must remain in its Place wherein it was apprehended in its Creation and formed into an Image, and not depart out of that same Harmony, or else it becomes an Enemy of the Being of all Beings.

23. And thus Hell is even an Enemy of the Devil, for he is a strange guest therein, *viz.* a perjured Fiend cast out of Heaven: he will be Lord in that wherein he was not created; the whole Creation accuses him for a false perjured apostate Spirit, which is departed from his Order;

yea even the Nature in the Wrath is his Enemy though he be of the same Property; yet he is a Stranger, and will be Lord, though he has lost his Kingdom, and is only an Inmate in the Wrath of God; he that was too rich, is now become too poor; he had all when he stood in Humility, and now he has Nothing, and is moreover captivated in the Gulf: this is his Shame, that he is a King, and yet has fooled away his Kingdom in Pride; the royal Creature remains, but the Dominion is taken away; of a King he is become an Executioner; what God's Anger apprehends, there he is a Judge, *viz.* an Officer of God's Anger, yet he must do what his Lord and Master wills.

24. This Reason most ignorantly gainsays, and says, *God is omnipotent, and omniscient, he has made it: Even he hath done with his* Work *as he hath pleased, who will contend with the Most High?* Yes, dear Reason, now thou thinkest thou hittest it right; but first learn the A B C in the great Mystery: All whatever is risen out of the eternal Will, *viz.* out of the great eternal Mystery of all Beings (as Angels and the Souls of Men are), stands in equal Weight in Evil and Good in the free Will as God himself; that Desire which powerfully and predominantly works in the Creature, and quite overtops the other, of that Property the Creature is. As a Candle puts forth out of itself a Fire, and out of the Fire the Wind, which Wind the Fire draws again into itself, and yet gives it forth again; and when this Spirit is gone forth from the Fire and Light, then it is free from the Fire and Light; what Property it again receives, of that it is: The first Mystery wherein the Creature consists is the all-essential Mystery, and the other in the forth-going Spirit is its Propriety, and a selfful Will. Has not every Angel its own peculiar Spirit, which is generated out of its own Mystery, which has its Original out of Eternity? Why will this Spirit be a

Tempter of God, and tempt the Mystery, which immediately captivates it in the Wrath, as happened to Lucifer? It has the drawing to God's Wrath and to God's Love in it; why does not the Spirit (which is generated out of both) which is the Similitude of the Spirit of God, continue in its Place in Obedience, as a Child before the Mother in Humility?

25. Thou sayst it cannot; It is not so: Every Spirit stands in the Place where it was created in equal Weight, and has its free Will; it is a Spirit with the all-essential Eternal Spirit, and may take to itself a Lubet in the all-essential Eternal Spirit as it Wills, either in God's Love or Anger; whereinto it introduces its longing Imagination, the Essence and Property of that it receives in the great Mystery of all Beings.

26. In God the Birth is manifest in Love and Anger; why not also in the Creature which is created out of God's Essence and Will, out of his Voice and Breath into an Image? What Property [or Note] of the Voice the Creature awakes in itself, the same sounds in, and rules the Creature: God's Will to the Creature was only one, *viz.* a general Manifestation of the Spirit, as each [Creature] was apprehended in the Property of the eternal Mystery; yet, Lucifer was apprehended in the good Angelical Property, which plainly testifies that he was an Angel in Heaven; but his own incorporised Will-Spirit forced itself into the wrathful Mother, to awaken the same in it, and thereby to be a Lord over every created Being. Now the Will-Spirit is free, it is the eternal Original, let it do what it will.

27. Therefore we are to know this, and it is no otherwise, that the Will-Spirit which takes its Original out of Love and Anger, out of both eternal Principles, has given itself into the Wrath, whereby the Wrath has Powerfully got the

upper Hand and Dominion, and put itself out of the equal Harmony into a Dissonance or Discord, and so he must be driven into his Likeness; this is his Fall, and so it is also the Fall of all Evil Men.

28. Now Self-Reason alleges the Scripture, where it is written, *Many are called, but few are chosen*: Also, *I have Loved Jacob and hated Esau*; also, *Hath not a Potter Power to make of one lump [of* Earth*] what he pleaseth?* I say the same also, *That many are called, but few are chosen*; for they will not; they give their free Will into God's Anger, where they are even apprehended, and so are chosen to be *Children of Wrath*; whereas they were all called in *Adam* into Paradise, and in Christ into the Regeneration; but they would not, the free Will would not, it exalted itself into the Wrath of God which apprehended it, and so they were not chosen Children; for God's Love chooses only its Likeness, and so likewise God's Anger; yet the Gate of the Regeneration stands open to the Wicked, whom the Anger of God has apprehended. Man has the Death in him, whereby he may die to the Evil; but the Devil has not, for he was created to the highest Perfection.

29. Thus it is also with Jacob and Esau: In Jacob the Line of Christ got the upper Hand in the wrestling Wheel; and in Esau the Fall of *Adam*; now Christ was therefore promised into the Humanity, that he might heal the Fall of *Adam*, and redeem Esau, which was captivated in the Wrath, from the Wrath; Jacob denotes Christ; and Esau *Adam*; now Christ is to redeem *Adam* from Death and Wrath, wherein he was captivated: But did Esau continue in Sin? That I know not; the Scripture also does not declare it; the Blessing belonged to Esau, that is, to *Adam*, but he fooled it away in the Fall, and so the Blessing fell upon Jacob, that is upon Christ, who should bless *Adam*

and Esau, so that the Kingdom and Blessing might be given of free Grace again to *Adam* and Esau; though he was apprehended in the Curse, yet the Door of Grace stood open in Jacob, that is, in Christ; therefore Jacob said afterward, that is Christ, when he was entered into *Adam*'s Soul and Flesh, *Come unto me all ye that are weary and heavy laden with your sins, and I will refresh you*: Also, *I am come to call the sinner to Repentance*; not Jacob, who needs it not, but Esau, who needs it; and when he (*viz.* Esau) is come, then says Christ, *There is more Joy in Heaven for him, than for ninety-nine righteous ones, which need no Repentance*; [*viz.* for one Esau that repents] there is more Joy than for ninety-nine Jacobs, who in the Centre of the Life's Original are apprehended in the Line of Christ: There is more Joy for one poor Sinner, whom the Anger has apprehended in the Centre of God's Wrath in the Life's Original, and chosen to Condemnation, if he brings the Sins of Death again into the Mortification or Death of Sin, than for ninety-nine righteous ones that need no Repentance.

30. But who are the Righteous, for we are all become Sinners in *Adam*? Answer, They are those whom the Line of Christ in the Humanity apprehends in the Life's Rise [or at the first Point of Opening of Life in them], not that they cannot fall as *Adam*, but that they are apprehended in Christ's Will-Spirit in the wrestling Wheel, where Love and Anger are counterpoised, and chosen to Life; as happened to Jacob, so also to Isaac, and Abel: But this Line should be the Preacher and Teacher of Cain, Ishmael, and Esau, and exhort them to Repentance, and to turn out of the Anger: And this Line did give itself into the Anger which was enkindled in Adam, Cain, Ishmael, and destroyed the Devil's Sting with Love, that *Cain*, *Ishmael*, and *Esau* had an open Gate to Grace; if they

would but turn and die in Jacob, that is, if they would enter into Christ's Death, and die to Sin in *Abel, Isaac,* and *Jacob*, and Christ, then they should be received into the Election of Grace.

31. *Jacob* took *Esau's* Place in the Blessing: Why did that come to pass? In *Jacob* was the promised Seed of Abraham and *Adam*; from this Line the Blessing should come upon the sinful *Adam* and *Esau; Jacob* must be filled with God's Blessing, that he might bless the First-Born of angry *Adam* and *Esau*; for the Blessing, that is, Christ must be born in our Flesh and Soul, that the Seed of the Woman might bruise the Head of the Serpent.

32. The Anger must be drowned and appeased in the Humanity; an Offering did not do it, but this resigning into the Wrath, that the Love might drown the Wrath. *Jacob* in Christ must drown *Esau* in the Love-Power in his Blood, that *Esau* might also become a *Jacob* in Christ: But *Esau* was not willing to receive his brother *Jacob*, and contended about the first Birth; that is, *Adam* in Sin will not, cannot receive [or accept of] Christ, he shall and must die to the sinful Flesh and Will.

33. Therefore *Esau* has ever fought against *Jacob*; for *Jacob* should drown him in Christ in his Blood; this the evil *Adam* in *Esau* would not have, he would live in his Selfhood, therefore he strove with the earthly *Adam* against *Jacob*; but when *Jacob* met him with his gifts, that is, when Christ came with his free Love-gift into the Humanity, then *Esau* fell upon his brother *Jacob's* neck and wept; for when Christ entered into the Humanity, *Adam* wept in *Esau*, and repented him of his Sins and Evil intent, that he would kill *Jacob*: For when God's Love in the Humanity entered into God's Anger, the angry Father bewailed our Sins and Misery, and *Jacob* with his

Humility drove forth mournful Tears out of his brother *Esau*; that is, the Love in the Humanity brought forth the great compassion out of and through the angry Father; so that the angry Father in the midst of his enkindled Wrath in the Humanity did set open a Gate of Mercy for *Adam* and all his Children; for his Love broke the Anger, which [Love] put itself into Death, and made an open Gate for poor Sinners in the Death to his Grace.

34. Now it is commanded the poor Sinner, whom the Anger has chosen to the Condemnation of eternal Death, that he enter into this same Death, and die in Christ's Death to Sin, and then Christ drowns it in his Blood, and chooses him again to be God's Child.

35. Here is the calling: Christ calls us into his Death, into his Dying; this the Sinner will not have: Here is now Strife in the Sinner between the Seed of the Woman and the Seed of the Serpent; which now overcomes, that conceives the Child: Now the free Will may reach to which it pleases; both Gates stand open to him. Many who are in Christ's Line are also brought through Imagination and Lust, as *Adam* was, into Iniquity; they are indeed called, but they persevere not in the Election, for the Election is set upon him who departs from Sin; he is elected that dies to Sin in Christ's Death, and rises in Christ's Resurrection, who receives God in Christ, not only in the Mouth, but in divine Desire in the Will and new-Birth, as a new fiery Generation: Knowledge apprehends it not, only the earnest Desire and Breaking of the sinful Will, that apprehends it.

36. Thus there is no sufficient Ground in the Election of Grace as Reason holds it forth: *Adam* is chosen in Christ; but that many a Twig withers on the Tree, is not the Tree's fault, for it withdraws its Sap from no Twig, only the

Twig gives forth itself too eagerly with the Desire; it runs on in Self-Will, *viz.* it is taken by the Inflammation of the Sun and the Fire, before it can draw Sap again in its Mother, and refresh itself.

37. Thus also Man perishes among the evil Company in evil vain Ways: God offers him his Grace that he should repent; but evil company and the Devil lead him in wicked ways, till he be even too hard captivated in the Anger; and then it goes very hardly with him; he indeed was called, but he is evil; God chooses only Children: Seeing he is evil, the choice passes over him; but if he again reforms and amends, the eternal choice [or Election] does again receive him.

38. Thus says the Scripture, *Many are called*; but when the Choice in Christ's Suffering and Death comes upon them, then they are not capable of the same, by Reason of the selfful evil Will which they had before embraced, and so they are not the Elected, but evil Children; and here it is then rightly said, *We have piped unto you, but you have not danced; we have mourned unto you, and ye have not lamented unto us: O Jerusalem, how often would I have gathered thy* Children *together, as a hen gathereth her chickens under her wings, and thou wouldest not*: It is not said, *thou couldest not*, but *thou wouldest not*; and while they remain in the Iniquity of Sin, they also cannot: God will not cast his Pearl before Swine; but to the Children which draw near to him he gives the Pearl and his Bread.

39. Therefore whoever blames God, despises his Mercy, which he has introduced into the Humanity, and brings the Judgement headlong upon his Body and Soul.

40. Thus I have truly warned the Reader, and set before his Eyes what the Lord of all Beings has given me: He may behold himself in this Looking-Glass both within and

without, and find what and who he is: Every Reader shall find his Profit therein, be he either good or evil: It is a very clear Gate of the Mystery of all Beings. With Glosses and Self-Wit none shall apprehend it in its own Ground; but it may well embrace the real Seeker, and create him much Profit and Joy, and even be helpful to him in all natural Things, provided he applies himself right, and seeks it in the Fear of God, seeing it is now a Time of Seeking; for a Lily blossoms upon the mountains and valleys in all the ends of the Earth: *He that seeketh findeth.* Amen.

HALLELUJAH